The Capitol Press Corps

Contributions in Political Science
Series Editor: *Bernard K. Johnpoll*

American Democratic Theory: Pluralism and
Its Critics
William Alton Kelso

The Capitol Press Corps

NEWSMEN AND THE GOVERNING OF NEW YORK STATE

David Morgan

CONTRIBUTIONS IN POLITICAL SCIENCE, NUMBER 2

GREENWOOD PRESS

WESTPORT, CONNECTICUT • LONDON, ENGLAND

Library of Congress Cataloging in Publication Data

Morgan, David, 1937-
   The Capitol press corps.

   (Contributions in political science ; no. 2 ISSN
0147-1066)
   Bibliography: p.
   Includes index
   1. Government and the press—New York (State)
I. Title. II. Series: Contributions in political
science ; no. 2
PN4739.N4M6   070.4'42   77-84771
ISBN 0-8371-9883-6

Library of Congress Catalog Card Number: 77-84771
ISBN: 0-8371-9883-6
ISSN: 0147-1066

First published in 1978

Greenwood Press, Inc.
51 Riverside Avenue, Westport, Connecticut 06880

Printed in the United States of America

10 9 8 7 6 5 4 3 2 1

To Sally

Contents

ACKNOWLEDGMENTS   ix

INTRODUCTION   xi

1. Mass Communications   3

Section 1. New York State

2. The Press in New York State   15

3. Politics in New York State   26

4. The Rockefeller Years   43

Section 2. Governors, Governing, and the Media

5. Legislators, Civil Servants, and the Media, I   55

6. Legislators, Civil Servants, and the Media, II   80

7. The View from the Press Room—The Capitol Press Corps   99

Section 3. Triangular Relationships

8. Legislators, Civil Servants, and Journalists   119

9. Editors, Aides, and Reporters   132

10. Conclusions   147

EPILOGUE—THE CAREY ADMINISTRATION   161

BIBLIOGRAPHY   167

INDEX   175

Acknowledgments

My intellectual debts are clear if, alas, not wholly discharged. I wish now to acknowledge my debt to the University of Liverpool and the University at Albany for research grants without which this study would not have been completed. I also wish to record my thanks to two former graduate students, Mike Bibbo and Larry McQuillan, and to Albany colleagues Bernard Johnpoll, Carlos Astiz, James Riedel, Charles Tarlton, Ben Schuster and, above all, Joseph Zimmerman for their time and encouragement over nearly two years. Equally I thank all my unnamed respondents, none of whom, I trust, will recognize themselves or be recognizable in the text. Naturally, the author and not his respondents has the responsibility for errors of omission and commission.

DAVID MORGAN
University of Liverpool
England

Introduction

The Empire State is large, populous, and heterogeneous. Several of its governors in recent decades have aspired to the presidency, having built, in some cases, solid reputations as innovators and competent executives. New York State legislators may now disagree strongly about the recent Rockefeller years and their legacy, but, mostly, they continue to exude a confidence in the ability of the State to solve some looming problems. The press corps at the State Capitol is certainly aware that it is at the heart of one of the five top-ranking news story centers of the country.

The politics of New York State have been marked in this century by a tradition of strong governors, exemplified recently by Nelson A. Rockefeller. In four terms as Governor, commencing in 1959, the latter presided over a large expansion of the State bureaucracy and budget, over significant innovations in areas such as higher education and conservation, and over construction programs for huge State office buildings and roads. The marble towers of Empire State Plaza are but the most visible monument to Rockefeller and to the expansion of a State government he strove to make a model for the Union.

The Rockefeller ghost still haunts Albany, many months after his departure and the electoral defeat of his successor, Malcolm Wilson. The Democrats are in the executive mansion and have a majority in the Assembly. Facing them, however, is a majority of Republicans in the Senate, a large number of whom can barely remember pre-Rockefeller days. The partisan division between the leaderships of the two houses, the retrenchment posture of Governor Carey, the near-bankruptcy of the Rockefeller-created Urban Development Corporation in 1975, and the continuing uncertainty over New York City's budget—all have given State politics a drama and newsworthiness in keeping with the State's tradition. The 1975 and 1976 sessions were wearing for leaders of New York State and their journalistic watchdogs. The period since Rockefeller is producing as much news as did the Rockefeller era itself.

A time of reassessment of future prospects—when unpalatable decisions have to be faced and when partisans of many shades seek to influence newswriters and, through them, the people—is a good time to examine the state of media-government relations in New York. What follows is an attempt to examine key aspects of the relationships between legislators, civil servants, and journalists. The spell of Rockefeller is slowly fading, and his legacy is in process of reassessment on all sides. As will be seen later, the impact of the Watergate events on the press takes the form of a general wariness of government. Conversely, among elected and appointed officials, there is some defensiveness over certain features of their past modes of behavior. Thus, media-government relations are marked by a fair degree of skepticism on all sides. Journalists at all levels are faulted by many legislators and civil servants for doing a poor job, either for not covering State government well or for not covering it at all. The bias of newspaper publishers, the lack of interest shown by television stations, the poor quality of reporters, and their willingness to be used—all are singled out for criticism by officials. Conversely, journalists are quick to criticize the efforts of both legislators and agencies to encapsulate them and often point to the lack of real public interest in State government. This lack of interest, they claim, reinforces the preference of publishers and station managers for heavy reliance on national and international news that comes in over the wire services and is, thus, already paid for. Since most of their remaining news space is given over to dense local cover, journalists assert, it is little wonder that State political news receives coverage that is episodic and, above all, marked by a tendentious, pervasive *local* perspective. State news is too often presented as somehow filling out local political news, not as emanating from a vitally important, legitimate, *other* level of government.

The setting for most of the actors in media-government relations in New York State is Albany, the State capital, a three-hour drive up the Hudson Valley from New York City. Not a large city, it may best be seen along with Schenectady and Troy, as part of a medium-sized metropolitan area of some 800,000 people. The State government is the largest single employer, and the *local* mass media, naturally, pay the State a great deal of attention. The rest of New York State gets its State news via the capitol press corps who work out of the press room in the capitol. The Legislative Correspondents Association (LCA) has declined in number since the early 1960s and now numbers about twenty-five full-time resident journalists plus a half-dozen assorted free-lancers who offer only specialized news coverage to banks, insurance companies, and the like. The larger newspapers—those in cities such as New York, Buffalo, Rochester, and Syracuse—keep resident journalists at Albany and supplement them by extra reporters when the Legislature is in session. The wire services, Associated Press and United Press International, have minimally two journalists each in the LCA, and these are easily supplemented during the session by reporters from their much larger Albany general offices.

The only television representatives in the LCA are two reporters from station WMHT at Schenectady, a part of the nationwide Public Broadcasting System (PBS), which covers State news in a highly respected weekly, statewide news program. Until 1972 the major networks kept reporters at Albany, at least during the session. Subsequently, reporters were withdrawn on grounds of economy. Network television had not been a large presence on the Albany scene, nor had it assured more State-level news in the networks. A newsman who sympathized with the dilemmas of television reporters remarked of them, "They were ruined by their deadlines—State news could only occur before 1 P.M. since the film had to be on the 2 P.M. bus for New York City and, by then, the Legislature was just coming into session." Whether true or not, the networks have not sought to return to Albany, even though alternative methods of film delivery have long been available to them.

The two dozen journalists who form the core of the LCA report most of what appears as State news in New York State. The various relationships between them and the agency heads, the legislative leadership, and those surrounding the Governor are crucial to understanding how and in what ways the political agenda of the State is presented and relayed to the public. These relationships, however, need to be set in their constitutional, political, ideological framework and, too, in the context of the overall situation of the mass media in New York State. Only then is it possible to move on to analyze the reciprocal attitudes and the interrelationships of those actively engaged in the Governor's office, the Legislature, and the agencies and departments—the government of New York State—and the press corps. To begin, however, it is necessary to discuss some of the literature on the effects of mass media in order to clarify the tasks that this study seeks to undertake.

The Capitol
Press Corps

1
Mass
Communications

Democratic governments must by definition seek to mobilize and maintain a level of consent for their activities. As the scope of these activities has increased in the twentieth century, so the task of generating consent has become more complex and more prone to the contradictions inherent in rising popular expectations. As governments contend with the parallel tasks of managing the creation of wealth and redistributing it, so too, it appears the stresses in democratic politics have intensified.

The processes of political communication among rulers, and between them and the ruled, are thus as important as ever. The importance of media in that process may relate much more to an elite *ascription* of importance to them than to *demonstrated* effect at the individual level. Elites within societies behave as if access to media and media intervention were highly significant, if not at times crucial, to their ability to manage their societies. Students of urban politics and policymaking of late seem to be showing greater interest in problems involving media. For some years there was a tendency to assume the effects of media, rather than to analyze them. Even recently, on the subject of the press and American national politics, one could read Leon Sigal's assertion that the *New York Times* and the *Washington Post* were "the central nervous system" of the American polity without finding much evidence or theory being adduced to support this statement.[1] Thus, writing of the role of the media in New York City politics, Sayre and Kaufman noted that "the whole tenor, the atmosphere of political contest is colored by their presentation and portrayals. While it perhaps cannot be said that the mass media are more powerful than other non-governmental participants . . . it is clear they occupy a unique position."[2] Both characterizations beg questions and indicate the need for research. Critiques of policy analysis, likewise, suggest a similar need. Philip Coulter commented that the assumption of much of the literature of policy analysis is that "social differentiation produces social cleavages, which in turn produce demands on government, which in turn produce various levels of policy outputs. Herein lies an inferential leap. How does a 'cleavage' make a demand? How does government respond to a cleavage?"[3] He went on to urge analysts to look at *how* environmental characteristics are converted into demands and *how* these demands are converted into forms of government and/or policies. Each question, of course, subsumes many questions. All suggest a strong prima facie case for researching the role of the media, however small one may believe its role to be in the process of policy making or, more generally, in the political process.

Large claims for the significance of mass media have not been lacking. The work of Innis and McLuhan illuminates the historic significance of control over the means of communication.[4] Jacques Ellul has speculated on the current *effects*—intended and otherwise—of control of modern communication systems.[5] More recently the anatomy of these processes has become a concern of the general public and, in the United States and Great Britain, of partisan politics.[6] Political parties and interest groups—two major channels of political communication—have been vehicles for demands for *improved* political communication, on the one hand, and for greater access to, or less bias in, the formal communications media, on the other. Such debates have usually generated more heat than light, but have served to focus public and academic attention on aspects hitherto neglected in studies of communication.

Reflecting on the societal pattern of communciation, then, as did Richard Rose, we may wish to distinguish *vertical* communication —that is, communication between actors at different levels (for example, a president and a voter)—from *horizontal* communication—that is, communication between actors at the same level (for example, two voters or two legislators).[7] Both modes generate a variety of questions.

Vertical communication raises questions about the legitimacy of regimes, governments, parties, and groups and the messages they send downward and receive (or allow) upward. Much political communication, of course, is conducted without benefit of mass media —it is private to government, party, and group bureaucracies. The mass media, however, are usually a vehicle for all vertical political communication at some stage or other. When they are used as a channel downward, there is the question of reader/watcher/listener attention and the use made by them of media messages: how can media be used by governments to reach citizens quickly, to inform them as fully as possible, and so on? Conversely, there is the questions of ensuring—in democracies at least—a marketplace for ideas, since governments easily dominate the attention of media organizations by possessing obviously superior resources of information and expertise, not to mention legitimacy. The questions in this area focus on how to enable actual or potential leadership groups outside government (*oppositions*, in the British sense) to reach their followers or the mass public. Similar questions of access to media occur when their use for upward communication is considered. How may the media become and remain open to dissenting views—for example, from ignored, alienated minorities? How can media organizations avoid becoming vehicles for "professional communicators"—co-opted by decision makers at different levels or simply emasculated by a desire to be effective by staying always in the so-called mainstream of ideas? In a more general sense, how can mass media be used to assist the process of agenda setting (the political surfacing of issues) in society when at all levels of polities there are likely to be disputes over what is desirable (that is, values) and over what is possible (that is, resources)?

In the area of horizontal communication, likewise, the private sector (intragroup and intergroup) is large, but sooner or later messages from it will seek out or find themselves in the public mass media. At the elite level, questions may relate to the role of media in facilitating communication between various elites, for example, the economic and the political. Again there is the question of media competing with all or part of the political elite in setting the agenda for the polity. Historically, the structured situation of media in the United States and Great Britain has been one of relative constitutional protection to allow them to engage in and be the vehicle for just such a competition, often to the chagrin of the political elite.

Such chagrin occurs because the political elites, past and present, ascribed greater actual and potential influence to the existence and operation of the mass media.[8] Nowadays this is true not only for communication between the elite and the mass, but also for communication between segments of the elite. For both horizontal and vertical communication processes, students of the media have sought to understand the process of communication and its effects. The near-classic model for some time was Elihu Katz's "two step flow" model.[9] (See Figure 1.1.) Deriving from the work of Lazarsfeld, Berelson, and Gaudet, this theory postulated that media primarily influenced opinion leaders at all levels of the polity—the first stage—and these individuals then influenced others by their face-to-face contact—the second stage.[10] Recently R. S. Frank has criticized this model, using the work of Greenberg and others to show that most face-to-face contact is noncontroversial; people do not "open up" to people they sense they may disagree with and are not easily persuaded to modify their views, even by friends. Frank concluded, "Working with the two step model, it becomes difficult to imagine how mass value and attitude change ever occurs."[11] He then went on to postulate that in the United States, whereas the press had long been popularly defined as partisan, this was less true of radio and much less true of television. The latter, evidence suggested, was seen as more neutral and credible—people turned to it after the press or face-to-face contact alerted them to new information.[12] Hence, in terms of attitude formation and change, Katz's model could be modified and expressed as in Figure 1.2.

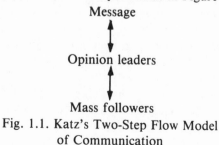

Message

Opinion leaders

Mass followers

Fig. 1.1. Katz's Two-Step Flow Model
of Communication

Solid lines represent reinforcement, while broken lines indicate new information and ideas.

Fig. 1.2. Frank's Modification of Katz's Model

For Frank television, particularly, has become an ersatz form of face-to-face contact, one that is very influential in shaping the posture of voters toward parties, candidates, issues, and so forth. Opinion leaders may still be influential in reinforcing attitudes, even sharing and strengthening a disposition to change some of them, but they cannot be seen any longer as the most credible source of information and attitude. They themselves are more liable than ever to experience feedback from actors who have derived their questions and, maybe, policy positions from the seemingly educative and more fact-oriented (as opposed to opinion-oriented) television.

All this leads to the important question of the effects of mass media. On this topic there is a great deal of ground clearing to be done if we are not to end in confusion. First, it is vital to remember that individuals—alone or in groups—are the *units* of effect. That is, when we talk of media effect, we mean attitudinal and behavioral changes in *individuals* that are occasioned in whole or in part either by messages transmitted via the media, but originating outside them, or by messages originating within them and molded by them. Obvious examples are the impact of pictures (the "visuals") in the "hot medium" television, or the volume of detailed information in the "cool medium," the print press. Second, following Seymour-Ure, we must bear in mind the distinction between primary and secondary effect.[13] Essentially, this distinction involves remembering that people—at individual and group levels —can be affected by observing others receive messages; that is, they draw conclusions about the intentions of the senders and the impact of the message on the receiver or receivers. This may be illustrated as in Figure 1.3.

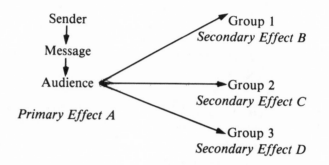

Fig. 1.3. Primary and Secondary Communication Effects

The effects will, of course, be changes in attitude or behavior by groups outside the primary communication, and these changes will relate to assumptions about the message and its significance for sender and receiver. Secondary effects may occur even when these assumptions are proved partly or wholly incorrect. For example, in the international arena following an incident between states A and B, state C and D may mobilize their military forces because they expect states A and B to do so and may then find their expectations wholly unfounded.

In the realm of the politician the primary/secondary distinction is important for a number of reasons. The assumptions made by actors about each other are implicit in conduct and comment and are explicit, inter alia, in constitutions and conventions governing formal relationships between the legislative, judicial, and executive branches and between all three and the mass media. Relationships between the judicial branch and the media are more constrained by notions of deference, contempt of court, and so on than are those between the media and the other branches; it is on the latter that I will concentrate. Patterns of primary communication may be illustrated in the form of a triangular relationship, as in Figure 1.4.

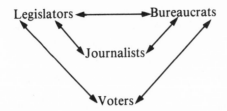

Fig. 1.4. Primary Effect Pattern

Legislators, bureaucrats, and journalists, as shown, communicate with each other and separately with the public. Patterns of secondary effect evolve from this, will reflect a variety of assumptions made about various actions, and may be illustrated as in Figure 1.5.

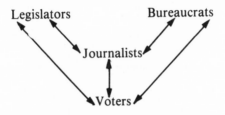

Fig. 1.5. Secondary Effect Pattern

Legislators pass messages to journalists (primary communication) and have the resultant publicity (an effect) interpreted by bureaucrats (secondary effect), and vice versa. In other words, the two groups may address each other through the third party of journalists, or even of voters (elections, polls). *Address* here is meant to indicate the element of deliberate intent. Thus, if Legislator A says X to Newspaper B, then Bureaucrat C is likely to conclude that Y consequence is about to happen and will behave accordingly.

Between these groups (horizontal communication) and between them and voters, clients, or readers (vertical communication) there exists a web of assumptions and patterns of behavior. Socialized into these and cherishing their distinctive spheres, the actors have fine-tuned antennae to what they see as changes in the relationships between them, an index of which is the volume and nature of communications between them.

Media-government relations, and perceptions of role as part of them, are the focus of this study. Taking New York State as its focus, it attempts to examine the patterns of communication between the Legislature, the executive, and the agencies and to compare their views of the proper and actual roles of the media with media views of their own role and performance. The study focuses chiefly on primary communication between the political, bureaucratic, and journalistic elites, who are physically close to each other in Albany, and the secondary communications and effects within their triangular relationship. It also looks at the assessments of those relationships made by public relations aides in Albany and by news editors far away at newspapers and at television and radio stations.

The basis of the study is information derived from structured and unstructured interviews with a 15 percent sample of legislators, (n = 32), a 10 percent sample of senior civil servants (n = 28), and the entire full-time capitol press corps (n = 24). In addition, there was data from a mail questionnaire sent to news editors and from interviews with fifteen very senior public relations aides working in the Governor's office, the Legislature, and the agencies. The interviews were conducted from December 1974 through March 1976, a period that turned out to be traumatic for both New York State and New York City. Extending over the whole period, the interviews allow glimpses of changing perceptions as crises intensified. Before the data is analyzed, however, there is a need to set these actors in their context, first, within the mass media and, second, within the politics and government of New York State.

NOTES

1. Leon V. Sigal, *Reporters and Officials: The organization and politics of newsmaking* (Lexington, Mass.: D. C. Heath, 1973).
2. Wallace A. Sayre and Herbert Kaufman, *Governing New York City: Politics in the Metropolis* (New York: W. W. Norton, 1965), p. 81.
3. Philip B. Coulter, "Comparative Community Politics and Public Policy: Problems in Theory and Research," in David R. Morgan and Samual A. Kirkpatrick, eds., *Urban Policy Analysis: A Systems Approach* (Glencoe, Ill.: Free Press, 1972), p. 372.
4. Harold A. Innis, *The Bias of Communication* (Toronto: University

of Toronto Press, 1951) and *Empire and Communication* (Toronto: University of Toronto Press, 1972). Marshall McLuhan, *Understanding Media* (New York: McGraw-Hill, 1964) and *The Gutenberg Galaxy* (Toronto: University of Toronto Press, 1962).

5. Jacques Ellul, *The Political Illusion* (New York: Vintage Books, 1972).

6. Vice President Agnew's speeches in 1969 and the alleged, but never admitted, hostilities between the Labour party leadership in England and the BBC after 1967. The late 1960s interest in participation contained such a component. For a discussion of this in England, see Harvey Cox and David Morgan, *City Politics and the Press* (Cambridge: Cambridge University Press, 1973), chap. 9. In the U.S. and the U.K. there still exist various organizations contending to have an input into communications organizations that they regard as closed and hostile to them, e.g., the National Viewers and Listeners Association in England and Truth in Media in the U.S.

7. Richard Rose, *Politics in England Today* (London: Faber and Faber, 1975).

8. Colin Seymour-Ure, *The Political Impact of Mass Media* (Beverly Hills, Calif.: Sage Publications, 1974), chaps. 4-9.

9. Elihu Katz, "Two Step Flow of Communication," *Public Opinion Quarterly* 21 (1957): pp. 61-78.

10. B. Berelson, H. Gaudet, and P. F. Lazarsfeld, *The People's Choice* (New York: Columbia University Press, 1948). Also Robert K. Merton, *Mass Persuasion: The Social Psychology of a War Bond Drive* (New York: Harper, 1946); and Elihu Katz and Paul F. Lazarsfeld, *Personal Influence* (Glencoe, Ill.: Free Press, 1955).

11. Robert Shelby Frank, *Message Dimension of Televison News* (Lexington, Mass.: Lexington Books, 1973), p. 11. For a review of the literature, see W. Weiss, "Effects of the Mass Media of Communication," in G. Lindzey and E. Aronson, eds., *The Handbook of Social Psychology,* 5 vols., vol. 5, 2d ed. (Reading, Mass.: Addison-Wesley, 1968), pp. 156-61. B. S. Greenberg, "Dimensions of Informal Communication," in W. A. Danielson, ed., *Paul J. Deutschmann Memorial Papers in Mass Communications Research* (Cincinnati: Scripps-Howard Research, 1963), pp. 35-43.

12. Frank, *Message Dimension of Television News,* p. 11. See also Jay Blumler and Denis McQuail, *Television in Politics* (Chicago: University of Chicago Press, 1963).

13. Seymour-Ure, *Political Impact of Mass Media,* chaps. 1-2. For a case study of primary versus secondary effects in the international system, see "The Times and the Appeasement of Hitler" in ibid., pp. 67-99.

Section 1

NEW YORK STATE

2

The Press
in New York State

New York State is well served by the mass media. As it embraces
the nerve center of the American economy and the hub of a vital
region politically, economically, socially, and intellectually, this is
hardly surprising. In terms of newspapers and radio/television stations located in the State—ignoring those serving it from neighbor-
ing states or Canada—New York State has 88 daily newspapers, 34
television stations, and 274 AM or FM radio stations. Behind the
daily newspapers lies a network of 569 weekly newspapers with an
additional 5 biweeklies and 13 semiweeklies.

Table 2.1 shows the concentration of the media in the cities of
the State and reveals the importance of the New York City area in
which are based the three largest newspapers (in terms of circulation), over one-quarter of the State's television stations, and one-
fifth of its radio stations. But numbers of newspapers or stations,
while impressive, are not the whole picture. Probably of at least as
much media significance is the fact that New York City is the news
center of the United States. The television and radio networks and
the wire services have their headquarters and senior editorial staffs
there, while the *New York Times* has something of a national elite
readership and circulation and provides its own important news
service. Only Washington compares in terms of the concentration
of journalistic expertise and news organization capabilities.

Table 2.1.   Mass Media in Large Urban Centers of New York State[a]

PLACE	NEWSPAPER	CIRCULATION	PUBLISHER	STATIONS TV	Radio
Albany	Knickerbocker News	63,000	Hearst	3	17
	Times-Union	78,000	Hearst		
Schenectady	Gazette	64,000	Daily Gazette Co.		
Binghamton	Press	70,000	Gannett	3	7
	Sun-Bulletin	27,000	Gannett		
Buffalo	Courier-Express	124,000	W. J. Conners	4	19
	News	278,000	Mrs. Edward Butler		
Rochester	Democrat and Chronicle	128,000	Gannett	3	13
	Times-Union	129,000	Gannett		
Syracuse	Herald-Journal	127,000	Newhouse	5	11
	Post-Standard	86,000	Newhouse		
New York City area					
	Daily News	1,926,000	New York News, Inc.	9	32
	Post	489,000	News International		
	New York Times	803,000	N.Y.T. Publishing Co.		
Staten Island	Advance	71,000	Newhouse		
Garden City, L.I.	Newsday	444,000	Newsday, Inc.		
Middletown	Times Herald-Record	58,000	Ottaway		
White Plains	Reporter Dispatch	48,000	Gannett		
Yonkers	Herald Statesman	46,000	Gannett		

[a]Daily papers.
Source: Editor and Publisher International Yearbook (New York: Editor and Publisher, 1977).

Historically, the New York City area has been of great all-round significance, for example, its newspapers, were for many years the only purveyors of much non-American news. This city has also offered a good example of a trend in media coverage toward concentration on local or national news at the expense of news from the state level. Only in the last few years has this been visibly changing, and the pattern of change varies considerably between newspapers, as we will see.

The pattern of ownership of both newspapers and radio/television stations is marked by chain ownership and by declining competition between newspapers in the same market area. Thus, the Gannett chain owns both daily newspapers in Rochester and Binghamton, while the Newhouse chain owns the two Syracuse newspapers, the Staten Island *Advance*, and the now-defunct *Long Island Press*. Similarly, the Hearst chain has control of both Albany newspapers, and the Ottaway chain, based at Middletown, is steadily building a network of smaller dailies and weeklies. New York City, with competing newspaper ownerships, is becoming anomalous in the State, at least in terms of newspaper ownership.

Political news—international, national, state, and local—is, of course, a product of editorial decisions in both print and electronic media. This study is particularly interested in State-level news, especially that carried in the daily press. Generally, at this level, it is true to say that the radio/television stations rely very heavily— often exclusively—on one of the major wire services and do not extend themselves even to supplement wire service coverage by much more than a repetition of their own local press coverage. That coverage, in turn, is the product of a dialogue between the wire reporters and a newspaper's own Albany reporters, on one hand, and its editorial staff, on the other. In this process how does State news fare, how much is offered to the citizen on a daily basis?

One must remember that each newspaper examined below claims at least a regional readership and so must try to give readers, for whom it is their only newspaper, a spread of local, regional, national, and international coverage. The cost of getting news is a real consideration for all newspapers. State, national, and international news comes in over the wire, and the newspaper pays whether it uses the copy or not. Local news involves employing reporters, photographers, and so on who, once employed, have to be paid whether their products are used or not. Bearing in mind the space available to them, editors have to consider, first, their fixed costs for news collection and, second, the need of readers for a spread of news. Political news at all levels has to compete with other kinds of news from those levels. In this competition the former has the advantage of perceived importance for the public, and in the minds of editors this advantage offsets the fact that they see its popular image as complex, abstract, and often dull.

Table 2.2 illuminates a variety of characteristics that give New York State newspapers their identities. The table reveals the differing size of the newspapers, from the tiny *Adirondack Enterprise* to the very large *New York Times.* Again, the figures reveal the different ways in which space in newspapers is allocated between advertisements, news, features, and so on. Even if one discounts the *Adirondack Enterprise* as exceptional because of its size and its wholly rural base and remembers that the upstate edition of the *New York Daily News* (as its low advertising total shows) is supported by the lucrative advertisements of the metropolitan editions in and around New York City, the range is considerable.

The range in other categories—that is, how space is further allocated—is even larger, and editorial profiles of the newspapers are very visible. For example, on a percentage basis, *Newsday* has almost as many advertisements as the Buffalo *News,* but clearly gives more room to political news and much less to general news, while providing more features and sports. The *New York Times* has an above-average percentage of advertisements, yet provides considerable coverage and expands it for all news purposes by cutting back on sports news and features. It is clear for all these categories that different newspapers across the State, for a mix of reasons (finances, tradition, preference, competition), make different decisions on how they allocate the space that their advertising and subscription revenues allow them.

Table 2.3 reveals how newsworthy politics is seen to be by the different newspapers. Here the strictly political news is computed as a percentage of all news after sports, features, and births, marriages, and deaths are extricated. In other words, how big a share is given to the political in the strictly news sections? On average, the answer appears to be that about 45 percent of the news is political in origin.

TABLE 2.2
Total Newspaper Content by Type

	Total News %	Non-political News %	Political News %	Sports %	Ads %	Features %	Births, Marriages, Deaths %	Total Column-Inches
Adirondack E. [a]	27.4	17.2	10.2	16.6	34.3	20.7	0.8	1,810
Albany K.N.	22.6	12.7	9.9	12.8	49.7	12.2	2.5	6,029
Albany T.-U.	18.5	10.9	7.6	8.7	57.1	13.6	2.1	6,258
Binghamton S.-B.	25.8	13.8	12.0	10.3	49.4	13.0	1.6	3,820
Buffalo N.	19.0	13.9	5.1	4.6	61.4	13.0	1.9	10,475
Newsday	16.1	6.4	9.7	6.6	60.2	16.4	0.9	1,810
New York Daily News [b]	36.2	14.0	22.2	20.7	2.8	38.8	1.4	2,118
New York Times	27.4	14.8	12.6	5.3	56.1	9.7	1.5	10,039
Syracuse Herald	17.8	9.2	8.6	7.0	54.2	19.0	2.0	6,243
Syracuse Standard	28.7	14.0	14.7	13.8	41.3	13.8	2.5	5,268
Watertown Times	28.3	18.0	10.3	6.2	47.6	16.0	1.9	4,692

NOTE: In tables 2.2-2.5 percentages based on column-inches; 5.8% sample; 10 February—2 March 1975, inclusive; excluding Sundays.

[a] 6-day newspaper.
[b] Upstate edition.

TABLE 2.5
State Political News Coverage by Functional Category

	A-I	A-II	A-III	B-I	B-II	Mentions
Adirondack E.	32.6	3.2	1.0	63.2	0.0	47
Albany K.N.	39.9	6.6	1.3	43.8	8.4	227
Albany T.-U.	30.6	9.0	3.6	54.2	2.6	210
Binghamton S.-B.	33.3	0.0	1.4	65.3	0.0	83
Buffalo N.	29.3	2.5	2.7	65.5	0.1	133
Newsday	50.0	8.3	0.9	39.8	0.9	108
New York Daily News	48.4	23.5	0.0	25.9	2.2	93
New York Times	30.8	8.7	1.9	56.7	1.9	104
Syracuse Herald-Journal	10.0	20.0	0.0	60.0	10.0	10
Syracuse Post-Standard	25.3	29.9	2.3	39.0	3.4	87
Watertown Times	35.0	2.1	0.5	62.4	0.0	102
Average	33.2	10.3	1.4	52.3	2.7	

tivities of legislators and bureaucrats, for example) and are put in column B-1. Column B-2 comprises items of a more informational nature: features, series, and the like that are not tied to a specific event.

It seems clear that few newspapers—apart from the Albany *Knickerbocker News* and the Syracuse *Herald*—provide much by way of background pieces on State government. Equally—discounting the Albany *Times-Union*—the level of supportive material is low. The bulk of coverage consists of straight news items on policies and personnel involved in State government and politics. The remaining coverage consists either of reports of demands made on the polity by spokespersons for groups of various kinds or of news and feature coverage of a kind that is clearly aimed at stirring the political pot at both elite and mass levels. Here noticeable variations in the posture of the newspapers emerge. The strikingly high level of reported demands (A-1) in the *New York Daily News* and *Newsday* suggests that the papers act as vehicles for publicizing of demands made within the polity. In the case of the *New York Daily News* this clearly goes along with an interventionist style of news presentation: it is not a paper of record, nor is *Newsday*, either. The Syracuse newspapers are interesting in that they too have an interventionist posture, but, unlike the *New York Daily News* and *Newsday*, they intervene not only by publicizing the demands of others, but by making demands of their own.

To get more of the flavor of a newspaper or newspapers it may be helpful to look a little more closely at one or two of them. For this purpose the two Albany papers are illuminating because they are untypical *only* in their concentration on State news. In their chain ownership, integrated news policy, and contrasting ideological positions they are representative of the mainstream in New York State.

In terms of newsworthiness it would be natural if the government and politics of New York State were to be more highly regarded in Albany than elsewhere in the State. The business of Albany is, after all, politics and government. As the skyline is dominated by the State buildings, so the society, economy, and polity lie in the shadow of the apparatus of government.

Both Hearst newspapers, the morning Albany *Times-Union* and the evening Albany *Knickerbocker News* are produced by the same

3

Politics in New York State

Warren Moscow, a prominent *New York Times* newsman in Albany in the 1940s, noted early in *Politics in the Empire State,* "Once upon a time there was a man who was elected President of the United States without having carried New York State."[1] The event has ceased to be news, but the amazed tone he parodied still had its echoes nearly thirty years later when a Mayor of insolvent New York City could tell Congress that he represented the world's greatest city and had exhausted the financial assistance of the greatest state in the Union. More than many of their fellow Americans may imagine, the local and state pride of New Yorkers continued to stand high. A state that had only recently been surpassed in population and size of economy by California could hardly be expected yet to feel itself second to any. Certainly this would be true of its governors, many of whom in the twentieth century have had presidential aspirations.

In the eyes of its citizens, New York State may stand high, if no longer highest, in the United States. Within the State, however, New Yorkers are no different from most other Americans in seeing their state government as having a less significant impact on their lives than their local government or, certainly, their national government.[2] In this respect there was a noticeable modification in New York City during 1975 and 1976, as residents saw a considerable degree of control of their city taken and kept by New York State and then by the federal government. It seems clear that, whatever the outcome, the reverberations of the current fiscal crisis will be with New York City, certainly, but with the State too, for some years to come.

A general review of New York State's history, while fascinating, has no place here. Broad surveys of its governmental institutions and their functions and an assessment of how well these are performed are also beyond the scope of this study.[3] What is needed for present purposes is to isolate the features of New York State government that are most directly relevant to the media-government relationship and, in fact, can be said to be the main determinants of its nature. If one considers the last three decades, these features are, first, the actuality of strong gubernatorial leadership; second, the extant style of dominant legislative leadership; and, third, the highly evolved apparatus for both executive and legislative public/press relations.

In the twentieth century New York State has had several governors—Hughes, Smith, Roosevelt, Dewey, Harriman, and Rockefeller—who thought of themselves, or were considered, as possible presidents of the United States. A recent paper shows how New York politics have tended to be marked by executive dominance of the Legislature.[4] While the first draft of the State constitution in 1776 had created a weak governor, an amendment was tentatively adopted, giving the governor an absolute veto. The Constitutional Convention, however, changed its mind and created a Council of Revision composed of the governor, the chancellor, and the judges of the Supreme Court. As a revising body with veto power, the council continued until 1822, when it was abolished and its veto power was allowed to go to the popularly elected governor. His term, however, was shortened for three to two years. The subsequent milestones in the advance of gubernatorial power were, first, the continuance of veto power in the new Constitution of 1840 and its extension by a voter-approved grant of an item veto in 1874 and, second, the approval by voters in 1927 of an executive budget system that gave the governor control over budget formulation and actual expenditures in a revamped administrative structure. Twice since then this executive budget has been unsuccessfully challenged in the State courts by the Legislature.[5]

record in Congress, he is well fitted for. The change may be nationally noticed for, as Warren Moscow observed thirty years ago, New York politicians—unlike other politicians at the State level—"do their stuff in front of enormous publicity mirrors that reflect their actions all over the nation."[14]

The second aspect of New York State political style that must be mentioned is the tight control over members of the Legislature by the leadership. A full account of the operations of that Legislature has no place here, but a few remarks are appropriate.[15] Gleason and Zimmerman, commenting on those operations, suggest that though "the strong executive concept is secure in the State in the foreseeable future, [the] . . . most significant trend in gubernatorial-legislative relations has involved action by the Legislature to become a full co-ordinate partner in the governmental process without eclipsing the role of the Governor."[16] Some efforts were made in 1975 inside the Democratically controlled Assembly to widen legislator participation and to weaken the grip of the committee chairs and, above all, the leaders on the legislative process. A Republican-Conservative-controlled Senate, economic recession and traumatic developments in the area of fiscal viability (for New York City and then for New York State), and dissension among Democrats—all combined to leave the situation essentially unchanged. Commented Stelzer and Riedel, "Each session opens with a passion for such reform, and settles for incremental changes."[17]

New York has a two-chamber Legislature. The lower house, the Assembly, has 150 members, while the upper, the Senate, has 60. Members of both houses are elected for two-year terms in even-numbered years. Generally, for policy and legislation there are few distinctions between the chambers. The Senate alone, however, confirms some gubernatorial appointments, removes judges on the governor's recommendation, and tries impeachments along with the members of the Court of Appeals. For fiscal year 1977 the Legislature employed 1,689 annual and 1,268 session employees and, overall, cost New York taxpayers an estimated $45.5 million. In 1975-77, some of those jobs came under press and public scrutiny: the "no shows," the marginal patronage jobs whose holders were supposedly rarely seen at Albany—or anywhere. Further, some of the legislative costs were under challenge, namely, the emoluments drawn principally by legislators in leadership positions in lieu of itemized expenses. These were the so-called lulus, which varied by rank and position and totaled just over $800,000 for fiscal year 1977.[18]

What, then, are the characteristics that help frame legislative activities and, in turn, media coverage? There is, first, the relationship with the governor, which has already been examined. The hierarchy apparent in that is matched, if indeed it does not breed, a hierarchy within each house; this constitutes a crucial second characteristic. To maximize their impact, the members of both houses formally delegate virtually all authority and power to act to the Assembly speaker and the president pro tem of the Senate.[19] These leaders then appoint majority leaders (their deputies) and chief whips, chair the Committees on Rules, are ex officio non-voting members of all other committees and of all statutory commissions, appoint chairpersons and members of all committees and important subcommittees, have considerable autonomous procedural powers, and, crucially, appoint all employees of their respective houses. On top of these considerable formal powers is built the superstructure of power and influence derived from their exploitation—power to grant or withold bill sponsorship, appointments, staff assistance, patronage opportunities, and, not least, capacity to influence the socialization of new members. The exercise of such a range of powers is, inevitably, conditioned by the need for consent, the need for delegation, the factors of party and custom, and perceptions of the overall political equation, actual and prospective. The successful exercise of such powers demands a high degree of information on, and sensitivity to, the needs and aspirations of committee chairs and, indeed, of committee members, often across party lines.

Third, despite the umbrella of a centralized hierarchy there exists the relative decentralization consequent on an elaborate system of committees and subcommittees.[20] Turnover of members is relatively high; there is circulation among the chairs but a fairly definite hierarchy of committees. If they stay, members clearly work their way not merely toward a position of chairperson, but toward the more important committees; the chairs of these form the secondary leadership under the respective leaders. The stability of mem-

bridged the formal separation between the branches and facilitated public policy formulation and execution.[24]

The fact of tight party control in a complex committee structure, with its resultant and frequent stresses, leads to much jockeying among the layers of leadership to decide what the party policy should be. Minority members and their staffs and dissident majority members are the providers of the endless flow of legislative news. Since it is important to have a say *before* the policy question at issue is formulated—far less decided—it is vital for all concerned to get into the act early, with as much weight as possible. In this process, members of the press are, and are very glad to be, allies of those wishing to signal a possible change of course or of those wishing to warn others that such a change will arouse varying degrees of opposition. In New York as elsewhere, journalists comprise a vital part of the central nervous system of the State.

As such, journalists are allies and adversaries of the public relations staff employed by the Legislature, the executive, and the agencies and departments. Together they form the third major aspect of New York State's political mode of operation that must be noticed. For a generation New York State government has employed numbers of senior ex-journalists—former editors or bureau chiefs at Albany—to manage media relations, write speeches and, at times, become general purpose aides to legislators, commissioners, and governors.

The significance of such high-paid talent is not lost on the leading political actors and newswriters in Albany—though all profess to be skeptical of its importance.[25] As alluded to earlier, one has to go back to Governor Dewey for the appearance of systematic public relations activity at Albany. Prior to Dewey, while governors might have sought to be the chief new source, no one had been so energetic in his attempts to muzzle other sources and promote himself. Warren Moscow lays much of this style at the door of Dewey's prior experience as a "racket busting" district attorney in New York City.[26] In conflict with actual or presumed criminals, news became a weapon—its ill-timed release could have adverse effects on a subsequent prosecution or could prevent an indictment being secured. Dewey thus made himself the only source of news and found it difficult to change his style when he reached Albany.

In Moscow's words, "he established in Albany the most elaborate public relations set-up the Capital had ever seen. Besides his own extensive secretariat, veteran newspapermen and speech writers were hired and placed on departmental and legislative payrolls to spread the Dewey doctrine that the State was getting the best government it had ever known."[27] To reinforçe the point the New York Public Information Council was established in 1946 by Dewey's staff with the aim of harmonizing press relations and the public information efforts of the agencies. Its secretary after 1947 was James Hagerty, the Governor's executive assistant and later press secretary to President Dwight D. Eisenhower. Later, when Hagerty became the Governor's secretary, he was succeeded as secretary by Harry O'Donnell, who himself later went on to work for Governor Rockefeller and Mayor John Lindsay of New York and recently retired as the director of information for Governor Hugh Carey. A study of the Council's work commented subsequently that "any analysis of the history and membership of the Public Information Council clearly leads the student of public relations to the conclusion that such a group would do everything possible to present the leader of the administration in a favorable light."[28] In the words of a critic, the council helped to make "Thomas E. Dewey . . . symbolize everything that was accomplished."[29]

Governors of New York subsequently have had this style as a benchmark. Nelson A. Rockefeller, after 1959, seems to have had Dewey's example very much in mind. The centralization of news supply within the Governor's office was quickly reestablished. Rockefeller believed that Governor Averell Harriman, his predecessor, had run a "slack ship" in this respect. Reflecting on the Rockefeller years, however, one of the most experienced Albany-based newsmen noted that the centralization of news supply was not total by any means: "The Governor announced successes, not failures." The dazzling effects of Rockefeller's tenure and the reactions to those effects will be returned to later. Suffice it here to point out that a study done in 1965—at the halfway point of Rockefeller's years as Governor—was revealing on press-government relations in New York State.[30] Edward Hale found a relatively high degree of acceptance of news management ("It's in-

ists and grand juries, New York passed a strong "shield law." Yet as late as 1972 a critic of the media organizations could attack their seeming lack of concern with freedom of information legislation, saying they "have done little or nothing to change the status quo."⁴³ This was after a freedom of information bill, having passed the Assembly, died in the Senate Finance Committee. Slowly, however, events were combining to create greater access. In 1969, in creating the Legislative Committee on Expenditure Review, the Legislature has set in motion a process whereby larger amounts of budgetary data would become available to the media: after 1971 the State Budget Division had to provide a revised five-year plan each year. The retrenchment after 1971 led to the creation by the Governor of the office of Inspector General of Welfare and of the office of Educational Performance Review in 1973. Both offices helped spread notions of accountability to the public by means of detailed exposure and publicity of policy and administrative failings. The Watergate episode dramatized the dangers of secret government at the national level. The result of greater accessibility to meetings and documents in this process was clear; legislators who opposed enabling legislation of this kind ran the risk of being accused of impeding the accountability of the branches of government to the people. Groups in the State who would make such accusations were forming. In October 1973 the Coalition for Legislative Reform was formed from the Citizens Union, City Club of New York, New York Civil Liberties Union, New York Urban Coalition, Community Service Society, and Women's City Club of New York. Later, public interest research groups were formed in New York City, Syracuse, and Albany, along with Common Cause. During the 1973 session the Taylor freedom of information bill, slightly amended, was again passed by the Assembly and killed in the Senate. Meanwhile, Assemblyman Peter A. A. Berle had introduced a "sunshine' open meetings bill.

By 1974 the scene was set for a more powerful campaign than ever. The Taylor bill was modified to please the press, which had objected to various overly large protections from invasions of privacy. Again the bill passed the Assembly and failed in the Senate. Meanwhile, both houses opened their committees to the press, and the Assembly began to admit all interested parties to such meetings. Finally in 1976—after changes in party control of the governorship and Assembly following the 1974 elections, after failure of the bill in 1975, and after much pressure—the Freedom of Information Act was passed. How effective this will be remains to be seen.

New York State government and politics have been marked by a strong leadership style. Governors cooperated with the legislative leadership in recent years, but were, generally, much better placed to initiate programs and dominate their implementation. In any event, governors sought and expected to get a large share of the credit for policy successes and tried to minimize their responsibility for policy failures. In both cases, they and the legislative leadership sought to keep the media at a distance until they had determined what policy was to be. At that point the mass media were expected to play a large role in publicizing that policy and a lesser role in delivering to them public reactions, especially if unfavorable. In pursuit of these goals, executive and legislative branches built up a highly professional public relations capacity that gave them, and especially the governor, maximum publicity. As seen by the press, it also provided a potential for the manipulation of the media, or for their co-optation. Precisely because New York State politics are as they are, the New York State press feels hard put to maintain a careful distance from government and the temptations it can proffer.

Currently the situation has several elements that promise some change in the area of media-government relations. First, there is the steady turnover among journalists—over one-third of whom are under thirty and nearly two-thirds under forty. More will be said about this later, but it must be noted now that deference to age and experience is not noticeable among the Albany press corps. Second, there is the question of the Rockefeller succession and legacy. The latter is currently much under examination, since the overextension of the public debt of the State and of New York City is laid at Rockefeller's door. In both cases the raising of capital via moral obligation bonds (which were not backed, as constitutionally required, by voter-approved "full faith and credit" of the State) is

28. Bernard Rubin, *Public Relations and the Empire State: A Case Study of New York State Administration, 1943-54* (New Brunswick, N.J.: Rutgers University Press, 1958), p. 116.

29. Ibid. The words are from John Mooney, then the Albany Bureau Chief of the Gannet News Service.

30. Edward Hale, "Newsmen and Government Men: A Study of the Interaction and Role Behavior of Professional Communicators Involved in the Transmission of Information from Executive Agencies in New York State Government to the Newspaper Reading Public," (Ph.D. diss., G.S.P.A., S.U.N.Y., Albany, 1966).

31. Ibid., table 37, p. VII, 17 A.

32. Ibid., table 30, p. V, 15.

33. Ibid., table 38, p. VII, 25.

34. Lee Miller in Rubin, *Public Relation in the Empire State,* p. 70. Quoted from Lee Miller, "Can Government Be 'Merchandised'?" *Reporter* 9 (October 1953): 11-16.

35. Stuart Witt, "Modernization of the Legislatures," in Connery and Benjamin, *Governing New York State,* pp. 45-58. See p. 50.

36. Ibid., p. 57.

37. Robert W. Englehardt, "Freedom of Information Law in New York State: Status and Recent Developments" (M. A. thesis, Marquette University, 1974).

38. North v. Foley, 265 N.Y.S. 780 (1933); *In re Mojica,* 8 N.Y.S. 2d 868 (1938).

39. Blandford v. McClelland, 16 N.Y.S. 2d 919 (1940); Greff v. Havens, 66 N.Y.S. 2d 124 (1946); Sears Roebuck and Co. v. Hoyt, 107 N.Y.S. 2d 756 (1951).

40. See 12 A.D. 2d 243 and 10 N.Y. 2d 199. See Englehardt, "Freedom of Information Law," pp. 139 et. seq. on this.

41. Englehardt, "Freedom of Information Law," p. 144.

42. Ibid., p. 15.

43. Ibid., p. 36.

4

The Rockefeller Years

Media-government relations in New York State must be set in the context of broader attitudes held by the leading actors toward government and politics in general. What is also critical is some understanding of the impact of the years of the Rockefeller administration on those attitudes. Governor of New York State for fifteen years, this is the ghost that continues to haunt the State agencies, the State Capitol, and, not least, the press corps.

Legislators, civil servants, and journalists were asked identical questions on the Rockefeller years. Journalists, in addition, were asked further questions relating to their professional reactions and needs. One-third of the capitol press corps saw Rockefeller in office over a period of at least five years, while the remainder, with one or two exceptions, caught his last year or two. Thus, while the perspective of the majority of newswriters may be heavily influenced by the received wisdom on Rockefeller, virtually all had some personal experience at Albany that allowed them to sift what their older colleagues had to say.

Members of the press have found some difficulty in emancipating themselves from the Rockefeller era. Nine-tenths believed that Rockefeller made State government much more significant and, vitally, more newsworthy.[a] One journalist noted that "he expected the Departments to create news for him . . . he made it easy on journalists." Another explained how Rockefeller dominated the

City. Democrats and Liberals are, naturally, much more reluctant than Republicans and Conservatives to agree that Rockefeller's years were a scintillating success.[j] Their reluctance has increased now that they have come to see themselves as picking up the pieces for some of those achievements, to say nothing of finding a certain number of skeletons in some Republican closets. Further, since the Watergate revelations and a new acceptance of abrasively investigative journalism, there appears to be a growing belief that Rockefeller was not merely a media manager, but a media manipulator. Four-fifths of the journalists and nearly all of the legislators, irrespective of party, subscribed to the view that Rockefeller co-opted the press in varying degrees and thus avoided the critical detachment or impassioned analysis given his predecessors and, certainly, his successors.[k] Journalists "were under his spell," said one legislator, while a veteran newsman remarked that "he was a charming person, a guy doing a good job, and we saw him like that." Another veteran at Albany confessed his feeling that Rockefeller "was not criticized as much as he should have been, perhaps because we thought him a cut above the average politician."

The larger-than-life quality exuded by Rockefeller undoubtedly assisted his press relations when he was in office, and his style has been an important reference point for reporters since his departure. One journalist who felt this strongly said, after a recital of Rockefeller's faults, "Give me him—newsmen have sensed a letdown; Wilson and Carey *are* a letdown." Others in the press room dissented, stressing the personal quality of Rockefeller's press relations, which, said one, "Wilson ended . . . abruptly." Further, they stressed the damage that the Rockefeller style did: "He formalized the relationship with us so that it is no longer possible to get to the Governor." The press relations screen was kept up by his successors so that journalists felt no easy rapport with either. On Governor Wilson, particularly, many Republican legislators held reporters guilty of writing the Governor "down" to compensate themselves for Rockefeller's departure. One Republican Senator, commenting on journalists, stated, "Yes, they're lost, all lost without him." Republicans and Conservatives were even more certain than Democrats and Liberals that the Rockefeller style meant more—and not less—constraints on the press.[l] Indeed, interview experience strongly suggests that for many Republicans the end of the Rockefeller era meant the end of the era of successsful management of the media. Under Wilson, they felt, journalists seemed to get out of hand and, as Republicans they derived no joy from the better relationship that journalists seemed to have with the Carey administration. Agreeing that Wilson had received a bad press, a Democrat provided further evidence of one of the ingredients of failure in media-government relations: "He had a terrible sense of timing; he appeared a bumbler. . . . he couldn't impress journalists." He went on to quote the scathing dismissal of Wilson (reputedly made by a fellow Republican) during the 1974 election campaign—the Governor's campaign style "was about as exciting as watching paint dry"—and noted with emphasis, "That's no good for newsmen."

Rockefeller the press manager and the image builder, in the eyes of some of his journalistic critics, did damage elsewhere as well. Said one, "He left a philosophy of public relations in the bureaucracy." For this newsman and for others, this was not helpful to the press relations of the agencies themselves, since they now experience the force of a greater degree of media skepticism than ever. From inside those agencies, however, the view is different and more complex. Certainly most civil servants shared the view that the Rockefeller era meant more news management and more public relations activities, and only a minority saw this as providing more access for journalists. Sixty-five percent of them saw the era as one of strong constraints on the press. Pointedly agreeing with their criticism, one noted that the extension of public relations "had opened up a credibility gap in state government-press relations." Under Rockefeller, said another civil servant, there was "a greater concentration than ever on the governor," and the agencies were kept on a tight leash. Some journalists confirmed this, one noting that the agency responses at times were "to use us to pressure him since they could get through in no other way."

Rockefeller's departure, then, meant a surfacing of much suppressed journalistic criticism of him, just when agencies began to try for more *independence* in public relations activities. The coincidence made journalists more skeptical of government, and agencies more sure that the press corps was incurably cynical or ideologically hostile. A new modus vivendi between reporters and all aspects of New York State government has yet to be arrived at.

g. Were there efforts to manipulate the press and media? What form did these take and how effective were they?

	Staff sanctions	News mastery	Charm	Other
Journalists	35.7 (5)	35.7 (5)	28.6 (4)	5.6 (1)

h. Did Rockefeller's activities change the newsworthiness of political news?

	Yes	No	DK
Journalists	90.9 (20)	4.5 (1)	4.5 (1)
Legislators	83.3 (25)	13.3 (4)	3.3 (1)
Civil Servants	77.8 (14)	11.1 (2)	5.6 (1)
Democrats	66.7 (10)	26.7 (4)	6.7 (1)
Republicans	100.0 (15)		
Liberals	62.5 (5)	25.0 (2)	12.5 (1)
Conservatives	100.0 (10)		

i. Did Rockefeller affect the news sensitivity of the Legislature or bureaucracy?

	Yes	No	DK
Legislators	83.3 (25)	13.3 (4)	3.3 (1)
C. Servants	73.3 (11)	20.0 (3)	6.7 (1)
Democrats	53.3 (8)	40.0 (6)	6.7 (1)
Republicans	80.0 (12)	13.3 (2)	6.7 (1)
Liberals	50.0 (4)	37.5 (3)	12.5 (1)
Conservatives	80.0 (8)	10.0 (1)	10.0 (1)

j. How far is it possible to characterize the Rockefeller years as a period in which NYS was "mobilized for necessary state governmental activity"?

	Strongly agree	Agree	Disagree	Strongly disagree	DK	Other
Journalists	38.1 (8)	52.4 (11)	4.8 (1)	4.8 (1)		
Legislators	26.7 (8)	53.3 (16)	13.3 (4)			6.7 (2)
C. Servants	23.5 (4)	52.9 (9)	17.6 (3)		5.9 (1)	
Democrats	20.0 (3)	53.3 (8)	13.3 (2)			13.3 (2)
Republicans	33.3 (5)	53.3 (8)	13.3 (2)			
Liberals	25.0 (2)	37.5 (3)	12.5 (1)			25.0 (2)
Conservatives	40.0 (4)	40.0 (4)	20.0 (2)			

k. Is there any truth in the charge that Rockefeller co-opted newsmen?

	True	Untrue	DK	Other
Journalists	82.6 (19)	13.0 (3)	4.3 (1)	
Legislators	96.7 (29)	3.3 (1)		
C. Servants	21.0 (4)	42.1 (8)	31.6 (6)	5.3 (1)
Democrats	100.0 (15)			
Republicans	93.3 (14)	6.7 (1)		
Liberals	100.0 (8)			
Conservatives	90.0 (9)	10.0 (1)		

l. Is it possible to discern a Rockefeller legacy in terms of press-government relations?

	More access	Less access	Co-optation	None	Other
Journalists	33.3 (7)	33.3 (7)	19.0 (4)	9.5 (2)	4.8 (1)
Legislators	10.0 (3)	56.7 (17)	20.0 (6)	13.3 (4)	
C. Servants	5.6 (1)	38.9 (7)	11.1 (2)		44.4 (8)
Democrats	13.3 (2)	46.7 (7)	20.0 (3)	20.0 (3)	
Republicans	6.7 (1)	66.7 (10)	20.0 (3)	6.7 (1)	
Liberals	25.0 (2)	37.5 (3)	25.0 (2)	12.5 (1)	
Conservatives		70.0 (7)	20.0 (2)	10.0 (1)	

Section 2
GOVERNORS, GOVERNING, AND THE MEDIA

5

Legislators, Civil Servants, and the Media, I

The American political system and its attendant myths mandate wary relationships between legislative and executive branches of government—and between both and the mass media. There is a triangular relationship between groups of different size, status, and formal political role. Each group, seen by the other, has a recognizable image and a coherence of attitude and behavior that appears, when articulated to members of that group, to be largely prejudice and indicative of a lack of understanding and sympathy with it. Thus legislators resent such descriptions as "publicity seekers" or "ego trippers"; civil servants resent jibes such as "overcautious" and "self-perpetuating" (even "bureaucratic"); and journalists are sensitive to ripostes such as "pushy," "brash," "ignorant," and so on. The fact that these epithets do not enter into face-to-face communications between the groups reflects their awareness of mutual need and a respect for civility—*not* evidence that they always, or mostly, understand each others' roles. The nature of their professions dictates that, inter alia, legislators need public attention, civil servants need prudence, and journalists need forcefulness. Too often these needs are overlooked by the groups in their mutual, if private, recriminations.

The New York State case provides plenty of evidence of such

misconceptions. It may be that many owe their origin, as suggested earlier by a Wisconsin study,[1] to the fact that the complexity of New York State government makes it more like the situation in Washington, D.C., than that extant in most states. Certainly the State's complexity and heterogeneity are recurring motifs in the conversations of New York State legislators, civil servants, and news writers. Other misconceptions and failures of sympathy may, however, owe their origins not to differences between formal roles, but to characteristics of those playing those roles. Differences of age, background, education, and job experience all may color the appreciation of how the roles are played.

The rapid urbanization of the United States in the thirty years since World War II means that a small-town background is likely to be rarer in people under forty than those in older age groups. Roughly one-fifth of senior civil servants and legislators had such a background. Surprisingly, given their relative youth, nearly one-third of the journalists had a small-town upbringing and nearly 40 percent of them were from another state. Upward career mobility for a minority had gone along with geographic mobility. Only one-quarter of the civil servants were born outside New York State, while for legislators the figure was 10 percent, perhaps not surprisingly.[a] Journalists, then, are more likely to have some reference point outside New York State. Since they are sent to Albany by newspapers from all over the State, they are, like legislators, more likely than civil servants to have a greater variety of reference points and perspectives.

Added to some difference of background, there are noticeable differences of age between the groups. Some of the senior and older civil servants are faced frequently with queries, and perhaps criticisms, from legislators who are ten to twelve years younger than they are and journalists who are normally fifteen to twenty years younger. Seventy percent of the resident capitol press corps are under forty, and 40 percent are under thirty. A quarter of them only are of an age comparable to most senior civil servants, 54 percent of whom are over fifty. While it is true that there is comparability of age between senior civil servants and the legislative leaders, over 80 percent of legislators are under fifty—and 20 percent under forty.[b] To be pilloried by a twenty-five-year-old journalist is one thing; to have to defer to a thirty-five-year-old senator must be harder to bear for many a civil servant conscious of how near retirement is. Further accentuating this disparity is the fact that a great deal of the actual contact with legislators will be via the medium of their staffs—who are likely to be younger, and often a lot younger—than the legislators themselves.

Differences of background and age are reinforced by differences of education. Sixty-five percent of civil servants had a masters degree (usually an M.A. or an M.P.A.), and a further 15 percent had Ph.D.'s. Eighty percent of legislators had postgraduate degrees, 50 percent having legal qualifications (L.L.B. or J.D.). By contrast, only about one-third of the journalists had any postgraduate qualifications.[c] The gap in formal qualifications may, however, be lessened somewhat by the fact that all three groups tend to have the common undergraduate background of a political science or history major. Generally speaking, however, legislators and civil servants have (and must be aware of) an educational edge over journalists. The latter's cries that both use (and abuse) special languages (legal or administrative) to obfuscate issues and points of contention may be true. Equally, it may be the cry of the generalist layperson when faced with the specialist.

Job experience may also emphasize this. Not only are journalists less specialized in their education (formally at least), but their job experience prior to Albany reinforces this. By and large, the journalists come from general reportorial or city hall backgrounds on their newspapers. Usually they are senior reporters with most of their experience on the newspaper they represent. They are and have to be generalists. By contrast, legislators have usually been practicing attorneys, often in specialized branches of law. A minority have a pre-Albany career of elective office (district attorney, mayor, or county legislator). In both cases their language and outlook is likely to be more specialized than that of members of the press.

Even more likely is this with civil servants. For politicians the narrow specializations of law school may be offset by the *practice* of law and deepened by political activity. But for civil servants there is a linear, social science quality in their education (B.A in political science; M.A., Ph.D., or D.P.A. in public administration) that is then built on by long years spent rising in one or, at most, two agencies. By the time such individuals are past fifty, they have spent more than twenty years in the State bureaucracy and are highly specialized administrators of education, health, transport, or whatever: they are, in fact, the very reverse of generalist administrators. Even legislative committee chairs often are, or must seem by comparison, only partially informed, far less expert, in their fields. If that is so, then ordinary legislators—perhaps especially if young—are by definition ignorant, and the average journalist must seem barely out of high school.

Constitutional role apart, then, there are grounds for hypothesizing that in New York State government and politics there is reason enough for the relationship between legislators, civil servants, and journalists to be prone to difficulty and misunderstanding. Remembering this, can one say that their attitudes toward the government and politics of the State contribute friction points and intensify friction when it exists?

Legislators, civil servants, and journalists were asked identical questions on State government and politics. Their replies give some indication of the general attitude of the groups toward each other and, hence, of the context in which mass media operate. It seems clear that both legislators and civil servants have a higher opinion of themselves and their activities than each group has of the other or than journalists have of both. Almost half of the legislators thought New York State was well served by its parties and politicians—liberals being more generous in this respect than Conservatives.[d] A prominent Republican Senator summed up much of the favorable comment by noting, "Compared to Washington and other states, we're a cut above," and a Democratic Assemblyman added, "We're better than the credit given us by the press." Half of the civil servants thought similarly of the service provided by the State agencies. Many stressed the contrast with the "inertia" of the government of New York City, while others talked of "integrity," one noting that there had been "no scandal in memory."

Criticisms of members of other groups were volunteered freely.

Ten percent of the legislators thought that the State was not well served by civil servants, and a further 40 percent saw it as only fairly well served by them—Democrats and Liberals being more critical than Republicans and Conservatives.[e] The terms most frequently used by critics were "bigness," "overextended," and "unresponsiveness," though the latter characteristic, one said, was "noticeably improving of late." Parties and politicians were no better rated by civil servants. Only one civil servant thought the State very well served by politicians; a fifth expressed guarded, mixed reactions; and a fifth considered the State not well served. About one-half saw the State as well served. One civil servant referred to "parochial, partisan politics," while another pointed to the needs of the State being sacrificed to "reelection . . . and the special interests." One quarter of the journalists saw the State as not well served by its parties and politicians, and nearly a fifth viewed civil servants in similar terms. More than half the press, in fact, described the State as less than well served by both groups. Frequently cited as criticisms were cases in which legislators obeyed their leaders "in return for a future judgeship," while agencies were criticized, as one newsman said, for being "too top heavy . . . [prone to] too many studies, high salaries, and less innovation." Legislators and civil servants clearly need to maintain their self-esteem, since each maintains a skepticism about the other, and journalists appear less than enthused by either.

What, then, of the future of New York State? Each group was asked to assess the relative importance of strong gubernatorial and legislative leadership in relation to current and future effective government. It is testimony to New York State traditions that all the civil servants and all but one legislator singled out strong gubernatorial leadership as the key factor. Republicans and Conservatives were unanimous on this. Democrats and Liberals expressed a determination to modify executive domination and pointed to signs of change in a situation in which neither party controlled both houses of the Legislature.[f] A Democratic Senator commented on the great need for the State to "survive Rocky's totalitarian instincts." A civil servant talked of the "degrading of the legislative process. Rocky was nemesis: he was the only leadership left."

Another sadly noted that even before Rockefeller, executive dominance had "destroyed grass roots policy input." The post-Rockefeller era left legislators feeling highly exposed to the scrutiny of the public interest groups, and a few left the strong impression that life was much easier when there was always "the Governor to blame for everything."

One of the reasons for this private political nostalgia is, no doubt, the increasingly awkward situation that legislators see themselves in. An index of this is the importance they, along with others, ascribed to the impact of the Liberal and Conservative parties. Four-fifths of the groups saw these parties as significant, and more than one-quarter of each group ascribed considerable influence to them. Republicans and Conservatives, generally speaking, seemed much more confident than Democrats and Liberals of their impact.[g] A Democratic Senator, who saw the State as having "almost a one-party system," welcomed anything that stopped "the leaderships [from] cooperating." Both Liberals and Conservatives were "paper tigers," said one legislator, but their impact had been "tremendous." Some stressed the effect on Democrats, others on Republicans; but most agreed that they kept both parties "honest" and, in the words of one Democrat, increased the significance of ideology "in organizations which . . . [had] fostered mediocrity." A civil servant wrote with feeling that the impact of Liberals and Conservatives had been to increase "polarization of Democrats and Republicans on major issues—good!"

During the long 1975 legislative session the party battle steadily intensified. In the protracted conflict over the possibility of the bankruptcy of New York City, upstate and suburban Republicans were joined by a small, but vociferous, band of Republicans from New York City. The rhetoric of the struggle, however, flowed along the traditional lines of upstate Republicans berating New York City Democrats, and vice versa. Indeed, party labels notwithstanding, such rhetoric fits legislative and journalistic perceptions of the true nature of the conflict. Some 70 percent of both groups feel the upstate/downstate cleavage continues to be a real and destructive force in the State's politics. The party and ideological division here is very clear. The only legislators who see the cleavage as a constructive force in New York politics were Republicans and Conservatives. A few Democrats and Liberals are inclined to see the cleavage as more rhetorical than real, though they concede its political utility to them.[h]

By contrast, civil servants, who are closer to actual policy than to rhetoric, are less inclined to see the rivalry as real and destructive (44 percent) and more inclined to put it at the level of rhetoric (22 percent). One of the civil servants who did so, nevertheless, could not resist the comment on New York City that "it *is* a different world down there." The urban/rural cleavage, which mostly parallels the upstate/downstate cleavage, is seen by all groups as of declining importance. Interestingly, journalists (70 percent) seem to regard it as more significant and destructive than either politicians (47 percent) or civil servants (39 percent)—both groups showing a higher propensity than journalists to regard it as more rhetorical than real. As earlier, however, Republicans and Conservatives deplored this feature the least—or were much less clear about its effects—than were Democrats and Liberals. Along both these lines of cleavage the conflict of ideology is clearly visible. The Democrats seem to regard the upstate/downstate conflict as forced on them by their opponents and, as such, unfortunate. The Republican position, too, stresses that the conflict was not sought by them, but they do not deplore it as much, because they think that, overall, the State is the beneficiary of it.

The perceptions of conflict, actual or potential, are clear when the groups were asked about changes they saw coming in the politics of the State, if any. All three groups, but especially legislators (77 percent,) expected significant changes, usually along lines either of more two-party competition statewide or of a situation in which issues will dominate and change party allegiances. Republicans and Conservatives were more concerned to stress the former; Democrats and Liberals, the latter.[i] Indeed, interview experience suggests that fiscal crises after 1975 made Democrats and Liberals gloomy because of their social implications, whereas those very implications made Republicans and Conservatives gloomy because of the perceived political consequences—hence their fears of "a one-party state." Journalists were the most skeptical of likely change—nearly 40 percent saw few or none en route—and were least likely to believe that change would take the form of new, realigning political issues. Having neither to be reelected nor to stand or fall by programs, journalists seem much more likely to regard perceptions of considerable change as either self-serving or deluded. For themselves they are on the side of a weary "plus ça change. . . . " As one of them put it, there will be little change because the politics of New York State are "a natural situation."

Where in all this stand the media and their roles? All three groups have an interest in the views of voters on the operations of State government, and all were asked identical questions on the roles and effects of the mass media in that government. First, there was the contextual question of how significant did they think State news was, compared with local and Washington news, in *voters'* minds. Nearly four-fifths of legislators and journalists believed that State-level news was overshadowed by both. Democrats and Liberals—no doubt reflecting a New York City perception—were more sure of this than were Republicans and Conservatives.[j] "It's not sexy like Washington news, and that's a pity because it's the last level of government people can really comprehend before the billions of dollars are too many," said one journalist. A downstate Democrat made the same point, adding sadly, "As a level of government, it is not understood." Civil servants, again, mostly living in Albany and not needing to be so conscious of the day-to-day importance of news (or defining it differently), were less sure that State news was so overshadowed, but even they thought so by a majority of 55 percent.

State news, then, is in a situation in which it has to compete strongly for voter attention, or at least its producers think so. In that process the attitudes of those within the media are significant. That leading legislators and civil servants regard this as axiomatic as is clear from their replies to a variety of subsequent questions. Both groups see the media as playing large and ongoing roles in the politics of the State—more so among politicians than among journalists themselves (87 percent versus 70 percent).[k] "They are the only window the public has on the State level," commented one Republican. More jaundiced, a New York City Democrat noted that journalists "make heroes, plant stories, leak things that have no bearing, and then retract." An experienced newsman stated that the press can "build or destroy men and issues subtly over time," but another insisted that "we have impact only on appearance . . . not substance," though promptly avowing that "politicians think we're important." Journalists ranked the print press above television in terms of mass influence, but civil servants and legislators were much less clear. More Democrats and Liberals than Republicans and Conservatives considered television to be more significant than the press, though all groups were divided, feeling that television's influence depended on the issue in question.[1] It's "a headline service only," said an upstate journalist on the role of television. A downstate Democrat saw it as decisive because "it is fast, accurate, visible, and has no third-party distortion." A civil servant saw the print press as having influence only on local elections, since its statewide influence had been "preempted by television." A New York City Democrat noted that the city "has no real Albany cover. . . . [It] doesn't know what goes on and how important it is to influence it."

A further index of media influence may be the estimates of the role of the press in the processes of securing nominations and winning elections. On this question, of course, civil servants are professionally involved only when they see their own areas of interest being used for electoral purposes by politicians and journalists. Their views on press influence are interesting because they are not as *personally* involved. Further, more than the other two groups, they have been most exposed to political science literature and to its skepticism of media effect on voters. Like the others, they have mixed feelings about press influence on nominations, but, unlike the others, they are not convinced that press influence is large in the winning of elections. Whereas three-quarters of journalists and legislators accord the press a large influence on elections, only about half the civil servants do so.

Such statistics may reflect one important aspect of press influence, namely, its capacity to *seem* important, whatever its real importance might be. The press may be very important politically if the political elite ascribes importance and significance to it, and in

New York State it clearly does. Within that elite it is apparent that there are differences in the degree of importance ascribed to the press, differences no doubt related to the mobilizational needs of politicians as much as any variation in the "quality" of the press. Democrats and Liberals are much more ready to ascribe large influence to the press, both in nominating and electing candidates. For Liberals, especially, the unanimous response on election importance reflects the ideological basis of their party and its chief context—a huge city population in which the "nerves of the media" may be the most important means of communication between its members.[m]

The question of the statewide picture was made clearer when the groups were asked to rank order newspapers in terms of their mass influence. The New York City newspapers were promptly singled out by virtue of the size of their readership and, in the case of the *New York Times,* by virtue of its agenda-setting capacity and prestige. Interestingly, civil servants and legislators seemed more sure of this than journalists themselves. Nearly a third of politicians and newswriters, however, and a half of the civil servants hastened to add that, north of the New York City area (that is, upstate), the influence of the *Times* declined sharply, with the leading position being taken by the dominant newspaper in each area of the State. Republicans and Conservatives were less ready to accord the *Times* pride of place than were Democrats and Liberals. From much experience, the latter group was ready to accord as much importance to the *New York Daily News* as were Conservatives and signficantly more than Democrats. "If you are here long enough," said an upstate Democrat, "then the *Times* is the one." A very senior civil servant noted that "the important one is the one the Governor reads; and went on to observe that "with Malcolm [Wilson], in came the *News*—not the *Times.* "[n]

How do the media in general, and the press in particular, exert influence? Where is the clout? The answers were unambiguous: whatever the capacity of occasional editorials or investigations, the most influential role of the media is the routine definition and creation of front-page, headline news. Headlines in all their forms, print or electronic, are more striking, achieve greater penetration, and help frame the posture of the readership or audience toward all other political news, including investigations. All the legislators, irrespective of party or group, and three-quarters of the journalists affirmed this. Editorials, claimed one journalist, may be "more enduring," but "it's our news exposure that's critical." Another journalist, with television experience, said of the significance of news exposure for legislators: "Let idiots talk; it kills them."

Civil servants stood in some contrast. Perhaps, as so many observed, because their agencies secured very little routine coverage, their view of its importance was more ambivalent. Nearly 70 percent mentioned it as the key area, but nearly 30 percent did not, selecting editorials and background articles instead. This must in part be a reflection of a world view which, in contrast to that of journalists and politicans, stresses the value of privacy. To journalists, news is news; to legislators, bad news is better than no news; but to civil servants, no news is better than bad news. For such people the perceptive editorial or the well-researched article or series is more significant and influential. It accords more with their view of what the media should be doing and also with their view of how they deal with each other. Legislators aided by conflict-hungry journalists, they implied, conduct the public business by bluster and posture: civil servants, in their own eyes, do so by rational and, above all, *private* discussion.°

At the end of the day, however, legislators and civil servants *want* the public business to be public property. Both groups, naturally, seek to manage the process of informing the public; both tend to see fair coverage in the media as favorable coverage, much as both deny it. Reporters are quickly socialized into awareness that they are the targets of strenuous legislative and agency efforts to secure coverage. Nearly four-fifths of the journalists believe that legislators and civil servants define these efforts as very important, and three-fifths of the journalists believe that they are often used—and themselves use the news opportunity—to fly trial balloons, to be vehicles for leaks from a variety of sources. One experienced capitol reporter noted how "politicians overrate their stories," but another felt newswriters pandered to this because "they see themselves as part of the team." On the other side, civil servants were frank to say that they used the press on occasion to counter "bad publicity. . . [and] to force political leaders to be responsive . . . [as over] nursing home charges, mental hygiene, etc." The press influence, claimed several journalists, could be decisive when through a leak newspapers publish "something the leadership opposes."

Most legislators readily agree that publicity in the press or on television is very important to their activities—Republicans and Conservatives being the most sure of this.[p] Yet, in contrast to journalists, only one-third of the legislators and less than one-sixth of the civil servants claim to see the media being so often used for leaks. Democrats and Liberals, who accord the press less importance overall than do Republicans and Conservatives, are more prone than the latter parties to see a leak or a "plant" in coverage.[q]

The efforts of both legislators and civil servants are often dedicated to managing their public appearances. Perhaps neither fully realizes that in consequence, for journalists, *real* news is *by definition* the unmasking of this stage management, the disregarding of the public relations activity, the forcing of the various systems to leak information, that is, news. Even when journalists routinely process legislative or agency news releases, the mold these are cast into—the "slant" about which the originators so often complain— is the "angle" that journalists themselves have sought and is *for them* the dimension that gives the public the truth about the information and the journalists their professional satisfaction.

The question of a journalist's angle on news brings up, of course, the propriety or impropriety of journalistic activity as seen by legislators, civil servants, and newswriters themselves. By more than two to one, journalists themselves felt they had an editorial, as well as a reportorial, role; and by more than six to one, they stated a belief in the possibility and necessity of keeping these two roles separated. For these journalists the media space constituted a legitimate opposition to and watchdog of government *only* if this separation were the case. Generally, they had no intellectual problems with this notion and were much more concerned to stress their failure to cover government adequately. Said one, "Politics is easy;

government is hard." "How do you cover a glacier?" asked another. The media was entitled to come out in a posture of total, unrelenting opposition, newswriters asserted, when there was legislative tampering with the democratic process. As one put it, "That is a more neutral way for the press to have a role. We see politicans seeking to preserve power and tampering with the means of replacing them."

Civil servants were in striking accord—more willing than journalists themselves to see an editorial role for the media and even more adamant for the maintenance of the distinction between news and so-called news analysis or editorializing. Legislators, by more than two to one were equally adamant about this—Democrats and Liberals being more ready than Republicans and Conservatives to allow the press an opposition role.[r] Of greater interest is the fact that by 55 percent to 45 percent they prescribed a reportorial role only for the media—one that did not allow television, radio, and newspapers to support politics or candidates or to develop their own policies. Republicans and Conservatives were as clear on this as Democrats were divided.[s] Liberals alone came out strongly for prescribing both a reportorial and editorial role. Thus, the watchdog image is the one preferred by legislators: the watchdog may bark on occasion, but may not lead its masters to an intruder or, by example and activity, drive the intruder away.

Such a role would be much too passive for most journalists, if indeed they could conceive it to be a possible one. In stating their preference, legislators do not have in mind their cooperative, passive local weeklies, but rather the big dailies of the State, which are often seen as an obstacle in legislator-voter communication and which bid, as one legislator put it, to be the "alternative government of this State." Half the legislators claimed to have had their "ability to operate" damaged by the press—Democrats and Republicans being more ready to assert this than Liberals and Conservatives.[t] By nearly three to one, legislators felt that the post-Watergate atmosphere had intensified journalistic skepticism, even cynicism, so far as they were concerned. Democrats and Liberals were more likely than Republicans and Conservatives to assert that the change among journalists has been considerable.[u] A Democrat referred to the "negative influence of media," which meant, he said, that "they single out politicians for destruction." Another, a leading Republican, referred scathingly to the chagrin of the *New York Times* over the *Washington Post* "coup" on Watergate and said that The *Times,* "to compensate, . . . [was] trying to get the C.I.A." Civil servants commented on the "atmosphere of distrust" and the "soiling of government," but on average seemed less embittered; one noted, however, the price for the necessary exposing of Watergate "may be too high."

Civil servants, perhaps being less exposed, were more sanguine on press-government relations. Less than 40 percent reported having been damaged by the press, and just over half thought that the posture of the media had changed very much since Watergate. In this both they and legislators contrasted sharply with journalists themselves, who felt by almost a four-to-one ratio that their professional attitudes had been greatly affected by Watergate. One stated that it was now "no longer impossible to imagine evil in high places," while another noted how it had helped journalists, by persuading editors to "put a premium on investigative reporting." Commented a third, Watergate revealed "the evils of pack journalism" and "persuaded us that I. F. Stone was right when he said 'all governments are run by liars.' " The era has seen considerable trading of accusations between journalists and politicians—both groups exhibiting considerable sensitivity. Civil service detachment on these questions may mean that the full blast of the "new journalism" has not been felt or, conversely, that civil servants are less imprisoned by rhetoric and image and more concerned with results, that is, useful media coverage.

In this context it is interesting to see the reactions of civil servants to the question of whether the media structure (local ownership, competition for local news, and so on) intensified local—not to mention parochial—popular attitudes so that political mobilization on a statewide scale was difficult. Whereas all three groups agreed with this as a proposition, civil servants agreed with it significantly less (67 percent) than legislators (81 percent) and journalists (88 percent) and "strongly agreed" by considerably smaller numbers—14 percent, against 42 percent for legislators and 48 percent for journalists.^{v} Agreeing with the proposition, one leading New York City Democrat noted, "I have become more of a State politician now, though I can't tell my district that." Another Democrat referred to the failure of "political modernization," while an upstate Democrat said, "We're not supposed to be delegates, but representatives and leaders." A journalist of long experience noted how *intensely* local coverage was the press answer to television and regretted it. When he was young, he worked on a small western rural newspaper: "The last thing the readers wanted was parochial coverage—they saw themselves as citizens of the U.S. and the world, not just their own backyard."

This chapter has surveyed the general attitudes of legislators, civil servants, and journalists toward each other. Political norms call for a wary relationship between the groups, and we have seen that this exists and may be exacerbated by differences of age, education, and experience. The uncertainties caused by the departure of Rockefeller are visible in the gloom of Republicans about their future and in the resentment of Democrats at their having, seemingly, to pick up the pieces left after Rockefeller. The mass media are generally seen as influential, especially at election time, and the press is still accorded considerable weight despite the growing importance of television. Yet legislators are concerned about media editorializing—posturing, they would say—and by the intensification of journalistic criticism since the Watergate episodes. At a time when the State faces a serious, statewide fiscal crisis, it is also clear that all three groups see the media as contributing to localistic attitudes that constrain the efforts of legislators to help resolve the various problems.

Bearing these general points in mind, we can now look in more detail at the attitudes of legislators and civil servants toward the media. As these are examined, it is important to recall that attitudes toward the media are not held in vacuo, but, for each group, relate to its expectations of other groups and for itself.

NOTE

1. DeJmer Dunn, *Public Officials and the Press* (Reading, Mass.: Addison-Wesley, 1969).

DATA

Figures in parentheses = n
All others = %
Party Affiliation   Legislators only

a. Place of birth

	Out of state	New York, Big city	New York, Small town
Journalists	37.0 (10)	29.6 (8)	33.3 (9)
Legislators	9.7 (3)	67.7 (21)	22.6 (7)
Civil Servants	27.8 (5)	55.6 (10)	16.7 (3)

b. Age

	Under 30	31-40	41-50	51 or over
Journalists	40.9 (9)	31.8 (7)	13.6 (3)	13.6 (3)
Legislators		20.0 (6)	63.3 (19)	16.7 (5)
C. Servants		4.5 (1)	40.9 (9)	54.5 (12)

c. Education

	High School	B.A./B.S.	LL.B./J.D.	M.P.A. M.A.	D.P.A./ Ph.D/D.L
Journalists		64.7 (11)		35.3 (6)	
Legislators	9.4 (3)	9.4 (3)	50.0 (16)	18.8 (6)	12.5 (4)
C. Servants		20.0 (4)	15.0 (3)	50.0 (10)	15.0 (3)

d. Generally how well served is NYS by its politicians and parties?

	Very well	Well	Fairly well	Not well	Mixed
Journalists		43.5 (10)	30.4 (7)	26.0 (6)	
Legislators	10.0 (3)	43.3 (13)	46.7 (14)		
C. Servants	4.8 (1)	47.6 (10)	4.8 (1)	19.0 (4)	23.8 (5)
Democrats	6.7 (1)	46.7 (7)	46.7 (7)		
Republicans	13.3 (2)	40.0 (6)	46.7 (7)		
Liberals	12.5 (1)	50.0 (4)	37.5 (3)		
Conservatives	10.0 (1)	40.0 (4)	50.0 (5)		

e. Generally how well served is NYS by its present bureaucratic structures and its present patterns of expenditure?

	Very well	Well	Fairly well	Not well	Mixed	DK
Journalists	4.3 (1)	34.8 (8)	26.1 (6)	17.4 (4)	8.7 (2)	8.7 (2)
Legislators	6.7 (2)	43.3 (13)	40.0 (12)	10.0 (3)		
C. Servants	26.3 (5)	52.6 (10)	15.8 (3)			5.3 (1)
Democrats	6.7 (1)	40.0 (6)	33.3 (5)	20.0 (3)		
Republicans	6.7 (1)	46.7 (7)	46.7 (7)			
Liberals	12.5 (1)	50.0 (4)	25.0 (2)	12.5 (1)		
Conservatives	10.0 (1)	40.0 (4)	40.0 (4)	10.0 (1)		

f. What consequences in the present situation, if any, flow from the tradition of (1) strong gubernatorial leadership; (2) strong legislative leadership?

	GUBERNATORIAL			LEGISLATIVE			
	A lot	Some	Not many	A lot	Some	Not many	DK
Journ.	86.9 (20)	8.6 (2)	4.3 (1)	4.7 (1)	23.8 (5)	71.4 (15)	
Leg.	96.7 (29)	3.3 (1)		3.3 (1)	16.7 (5)	80.0 (24)	5.3 (1)
C. Serv.	100.0 (19)			26.3 (5)	15.8 (3)	52.6 (10)	
Dems.	93.3 (14)	6.7 (1)			13.3 (2)	86.7 (13)	
Reps.	100.0 (15)			6.7 (1)	20.0 (3)	73.3 (11)	
Libs.	87.5 (7)	12.5 (1)			12.5 (1)	87.5 (7)	
Cons.	100.0 (10)				10.0 (1)	90.0 (9)	

g. In policy terms what consequences, if any, flow from NYS having a modified two-party system?

	A lot	Some	Not many	None	DK
Journalists	30.4 (7)	56.5 (13)	13.0 (3)		
Legislators	36.7 (11)	50.0 (15)	10.0 (3)		3.3 (1)
C. Servants	26.3 (5)	52.6 (12)	15.8 (3)	5.2 (1)	
Democrats	26.7 (4)	53.3 (8)	20.0 (3)		
Republicans	46.7 (7)	46.7 (7)			6.7 (1)
Liberals	37.5 (3)	37.5 (3)	25.0 (2)		
Conservatives	40.0 (4)	60.0 (6)			

h. What have been the consequences for the State of (1) upstate/downstate and (2) urban/rural rivalries?

	UPSTATE/DOWNSTATE				
	Good/creative	Bad/destructive	Rhetorical	Unreal	DK
Journalists	26.0 (6)	69.6 (16)	4.3 (1)		
Legislators	23.3 (7)	70.0 (21)	6.7 (2)		
C. Servants	22.2 (4)	44.4 (8)	22.2 (4)		11.1 (2)

Democrats	86.7 (13)	13.3 (2)
Republicans	46.7 (7)	53.3 (8)
Liberals	87.5 (7)	12.5 (1)
Conservatives	40.0 (4)	60.0 (6)

	Good/creative	Bad/destructive	URBAN/RURAL Rhetorical	Unreal	DK
Journ.	19.0 (4)	71.4 (15)	4.7 (1)	4.7 (1)	11.1 (2)
Leg.	16.7 (5)	46.7 (14)	20.0 (6)	16.7 (5)	6.7 (1)
C. Serv.	22.2 (4)	38.9 (7)	16.7 (3)	11.1 (2)	26.7 (4)
Dems.		73.3 (11)	20.0 (3)		
Reps.	33.3 (5)	20.0 (3)	20.0 (3)		12.5 (1)
Libs.		75.0 (6)	12.5 (1)		12.5 (1)
Cons.	20.0 (2)	40.0 (4)	10.0 (1)		30.0 (3)

i. Do you see any changes in these relationships, and if so, what might they be?

	More party competition	Few	None	Domination by issues
Journalists	47.8 (11)	21.7 (5)	17.4 (4)	13.0 (3)
Legislators	43.3 (13)	10.0 (3)	13.3 (4)	33.3 (10)
C. Servants	38.9 (7)	27.8 (5)	11.1 (2)	22.2 (4)
Democrats	40.0 (6)	6.7 (1)	6.7 (1)	46.7 (7)
Republicans	46.7 (7)	13.3 (2)	20.0 (3)	20.0 (3)
Liberals	25.0 (2)	12.5 (1)	12.5 (1)	50.0 (4)
Conservatives	40.0 (4)	10.0 (1)	20.0 (2)	30.0 (3)

j. Do you think that in the public mind political news from the State level suffers by contrast with the frequency and immediacy of local and/or Washington news?

	Yes	No	Mixed
Journalists	78.3 (18)	4.3 (1)	17.4 (4)
Legislators	80.0 (24)	13.3 (4)	6.7 (2)
C. Servants	55.0 (11)	35.0 (7)	10.0 (2)
Democrats	86.7 (13)	13.3 (2)	
Republicans	73.3 (11)	13.3 (2)	13.3 (2)
Liberals	87.5 (7)	12.5 (1)	
Conservatives	80.0 (8)	10.0 (1)	10.0 (1)

k. How large a role would you say the press played in NYS politics?

	Large	Moderate	Small	DK
Journalists	69.6 (16)	26.1 (6)	4.3 (1)	
Legislators	87.1 (27)	6.5 (2)	3.2 (1)	3.2 (1)
C. Servants	78.9 (15)	10.5 (2)	10.5 (2)	
Democrats	87.5 (14)	12.5 (2)		
Republicans	86.7 (13)		6.7 (1)	6.7 (1)
Liberals	100.0 (9)			
Conservatives	70.0 (7)	10.0 (1)	10.0 (1)	10.0 (1)

l. Is it possible to distinguish the role of the press as compared with television and radio?

	TV more significant	TV less significant	Different	DK
Journalists	30.4 (7)	65.2 (15)	4.3 (1)	
Legislators	35.5 (11)	41.9 (13)	12.9 (4)	9.7 (3)
C. Servants	38.1 (8)	23.8 (5)	23.8 (5)	14.3 (3)
Democrats	43.8 (7)	50.0 (8)	6.3 (1)	

	Nom. Large	Nom. Moderate	Nom. Small	Elec. Large
Republicans	26.7 (4)	33.3 (5)		20.0 (3)
Liberals	55.6 (5)	33.3 (3)	11.1 (1)	20.0 (2)
Conservatives	20.0 (2)	30.0 (3)		30.0 (3)

m. What role does the press have in the process of securing party nominations and winning elections?

	NOMINATIONS				ELECTIONS			
	Large	Moderate	Small	DK	Large	Moderate	Small	DK
Journ.	30.4 (7)		69.6 (16)		78.3 (18)	4.3 (1)	17.4 (4)	
Leg.	41.9 (13)	9.7 (3)	48.4 (15)		74.2 (23)	9.7 (3)	16.1 (5)	
C. Serv.	33.3 (7)	19.0 (4)	28.6 (6)	19.0 (4)	50.0 (10)	20.0 (4)	25.0 (5)	5.0 (1)
Dems.	56.3 (9)		43.8 (7)		87.5 (14)		12.5 (2)	
Reps.	26.7 (4)	20.0 (3)	53.3 (8)		60.0 (9)	20.0 (3)	20.0 (3)	
Libs.	66.7 (6)		33.3 (3)		100.0 (9)			
Cons.	40.0.(4)	20.0 (2)	40.0 (4)		60.0 (6)	20.0 (2)	20.0 (2)	

n. Is it possible to distinguish between newspapers in terms of their importance in State politics? [Mentions]

	REGULAR READERS								
	NY Times	NY Daily News	NY Post	Albany	Gannett	Varies by area	AP	Others	DK
Journ.	38.0 (19)	26.0 (13)	6.0 (3)	6.0 (3)	8.0 (4)	8.0 (4)	4.0 (2)	4.0 (2)	
Leg.	41.9 (26)	21.0 (13)	6.5 (4)	3.2 (2)	4.8 (3)	16.1 (10)		6.5 (4)	
C. Serv.	47.1 (16)	23.5 (8)	2.9 (1)	2.9 (1)	2.9 (1)	14.7 (5)		2.9 (1)	2.9 (1)
Dems.	48.4 (15)	19.4 (6)	6.5 (2)			25.8 (8)			
Reps.	35.5 (11)	22.6 (7)	6.5 (2)	6.5 (2)		19.0 (9)			
Libs.	40.9 (9)	27.3 (6)	9.1 (2)			22.7 (5)			
Cons.	36.8 (7)	26.3 (5)	10.5 (2)	5.3 (1)		21.1 (4)			

o. Newspapers are said to play their political roles in a variety of ways. Place the following in the order of importance that you think each has within this role: (1) timing and the positioning of news; (2) editorials; (3) background pieces for educating the public; (4) the same for influencing the decision makers; (5) other. [Mentions]

	1	2	3	4	5
Journalists	74.1 (20)	7.4 (2)	14.8 (4)	3.7 (1)	
Legislators	100.0 (31)				
C. Servants	69.2 (18)	15.4 (4)	15.4 (4)		
Democrats	100.0 (16)				
Republicans	100.0 (15)				
Liberals	100.0 (9)				
Conservatives	100.0 (10)				

p. How important is it to you to recruit the press — or part of it — for one of your legislative campaigns? (For journalists the question was, How important is it to legislators and civil servants to recruit the press or part of it for one of their legislative campaigns?)

	Very important	Important	Unimportant	DK
Journalists	78.3 (18)	21.7 (5)	6.4 (2)	
Legislators	64.5 (20)	29.0 (9)	5.0 (1)	5.0 (1)
C. Servants	55.0 (11)	35.0 (7)	5.0 (1)	
Democrats	50.0 (8)	43.8 (7)	6.3 (1)	
Republicans	80.0 (12)	13.3 (2)	6.7 (1)	
Liberals	66.7 (6)	22.2 (2)	11.1 (1)	
Conservatives	70.0 (7)	20.0 (2)	10.0 (1)	

q. How often are you aware that the press is being used to fly a trial balloon?

	Often	Sometimes	Never	DK
Journalists	56.5 (13)	43.5 (10)		
Legislators	35.5 (11)	58.1 (18)	3.2 (1)	3.2 (1)
C. Servants	14.3 (3)	57.1 (12)	4.7 (1)	23.8 (5)
Democrats	43.8 (7)	50.0 (8)	6.3 (1)	
Republicans	26.7 (4)	66.7 (10)		6.7 (1)
Liberals	66.7 (6)	22.2 (2)	11.1 (1)	
Conservatives	10.0 (1)	80.0 (8)		10.0 (1)

r. How far do you think it is legitimate for the press to play the role of an opposition, promoting candidates and policies or leading and stimulating public opinion?

	Legitimate if news/ editorials separated	Illegitimate	Always legitimate
Journalists	82.6 (19)	13.0 (3)	4.3 (1)
Legislators	70.0 (21)	30.0 (9)	
C. Servants	80.0 (16)	20.0 (4)	
Democrats	80.0 (12)	20.0 (3)	
Republicans	60.0 (9)	40.0 (6)	
Liberals	75.0 (6)	25.0 (2)	
Conservatives	60.0 (6)	40.0 (4)	

s. In general what role(s) do you think the media should play in NY politics?

	News reporting	News reporting and editorializing	Other
Journalists	30.4 (7)	69.6 (16)	
Legislators	54.8 (17)	45.1 (14)	
C. Servants	21.0 (4)	78.9 (15)	

	News reporting	News reporting and editorializing	Other (cont.)
Democrats	50.0 (8)	50.0 (8)	
Republicans	60.0 (9)	40.0 (6)	
Liberals	33.3 (3)	66.7 (6)	
Conservatives	60.0 (6)	40.0 (4)	

t. Has your ability to operate ever been damaged by the press?

	Yes	No	DK
Legislators	48.3 (14)	48.3 (14)	3.4 (1)
C. Servants	38.1 (8)	61.9 (13)	
Democrats	46.7 (7)	53.3 (8)	
Republicans	50.0 (7)	42.9 (6)	7.1 (1)
Liberals	37.5 (3)	62.5 (5)	
Conservatives	33.3 (3)	55.6 (5)	11.1 (1)

u. In this respect how far has "Watergate and all that" influenced journalists?

	Much	Some	Not at all	Influenced voters
Journalists	78.3 (18)	21.7 (5)		
Legislators	72.4 (21)	27.5 (8)		
C. Servants	52.4 (11)	33.3 (7)	4.7 (1)	9.5 (2)
Democrats	80.0 (12)	13.3 (2)		
Republicans	60.0 (9)	40.0 (6)		
Liberals	87.5 (7)	12.5 (1)		6.7 (1)
Conservatives	60.0 (6)	40.0 (4)		

v. Do you think the locally based ownership of the media reinforces parochial attitudes and makes statewide perspectives difficult to maintain in the electorate?

	Strongly agree	Agree	Disagree	Strongly disagree	Mixed
Journalists	47.8 (11)	39.1 (9)	8.7 (2)	4.3 (1)	
Legislators	41.9 (13)	38.7 (12)	19.4 (6)		
C. Servants	14.3 (3)	52.4 (11)	19.0 (4)		14.3 (3)
Democrats	50.0 (8)	37.5 (6)	12.5 (2)		
Republicans	33.3 (5)	40.0 (6)	26.7 (4)		
Liberals	44.4 (4)	33.3 (3)	22.2 (2)		
Conservatives	40.0 (4)	50.0 (5)	10.0 (1)		

6

Legislators, Civil Servants, and the Media, II

Legislators and senior civil servants are busy individuals, but they seem never too busy to read the newspapers or, at least, to have their staffs read and clip for them. Both groups watch televised news and news analysis programs when they can, and the attachment to the print press and the element of love/hate in the relationship is often visible among them. What newspapers these men and women read and what television they view, together form an important element in their general world view, helping them to assess the competence of the statewide press and its relevance to the governing of New York State. These groups are highly specialized publics; indeed, they are very often the actors about whom the press writes and on whom the electronic media descend for filmed or recorded comment.

Legislators cultivate journalists and are cultivated by them in turn. The more senior the legislator, the less he or she has to work for coverage and the more statewide that coverage is going to be. The average legislator—upstate and downstate—has six or more newspapers, weekly or daily, in his or her district and six or more radio or television stations.[a] New York City legislators complain that the city papers have neither the time nor the interest to cover State politics satisfactorily and contrast this with the perceived closeness of upstate legislators to their newspapers. For the legislator from the city the local press is, under normal circumstances, the weekly press; and in that he or she usually gets full, if not always favorable, coverage. Upstate the situation is different— there senators or members of the Assembly are more likely to know the editors of the newspapers in their district and, certainly, their representatives in Albany, if they have any. The New York City legislators feel they are mostly ignored by the big dailies; their over-exposed upstate counterparts frequently envy such anonymity: "They still get away with murder down there," as one put it. Most legislators are happiest when dealing with their district press, though some complain that the reporters were not very well informed on State politics.[b] The Albany press corps, commented one, was "too cynical," and another complained that "the locals aren't interested in Statewide perspectives, but in *me*." Others who had previously been mayors or district attorneys found the transition to Albany somewhat disturbing. One said of the different press attitude, "There they used to besiege me; now I have to seek them out." Legislative leaders, of course, become used to dealing with a much wider corps of journalists and note often that it is difficult to keep their leadership perspectives from obtruding too much in their dealings with their districts and, as one of them said, with the "local press boys there." Nearly all legislators have counted or still count journalists as friends or acquaintances. This does *not* mean that they are necessarily close to the *current* editor of the hometown weekly or daily or the current Albany reporter for those newspapers. Knowing both is not being close to both and, given partisanship, maybe the reverse. Legislators, however, have more than an outsider's view of the problems and constraints inherent in the situation of editors and reporters.

Civil servants are more distant from the press, even though they are, of necessity, much concerned with the perceptions of their agencies held by people inside and outside government. The way these are presented in the media can influence the attitudes not merely of voters, but also of legislators and, importantly, those around the Governor. Both for defensive reasons—program maintenance or expansion—and for offensive reasons—public education and mobilization—the image of the agency is important, and civil servants know it. They, too, have an element of "district" concern, since their responsibilities and activities are often concentrated in certain parts of the State. Civil servants might be located in Albany, but find themselves increasingly concerned with, say, New York City reactions to educational finance or welfare. Like legislators, civil servants are much more likely to count journalists among their friends or acquaintances (76 percent claim this). Here again, these need not be among locally based journalists or still active journalists. But generally, few senior civil servants are ignorant of the situation and needs of the press.

What newspapers do these groups read? The single most mentioned paper is the *New York Times*, which more than half of the civil servants and two-thirds of the legislators claim to read daily. The two Albany papers—the morning *Times-Union* and the evening *Knickerbocker News*—seem to be regarded as conservative and liberal editions of the same newspaper and are mentioned by nearly 40 percent of civil servants and by more than half of the legislators when in session. There appears to be little discernible variation by party or persuasion: Conservatives are as likely as Liberals to read the *New York Times* or the Albany newspapers. Outside these staples the spread of regular or "occasional" reading is considerable. Nearly a seventh of legislators and civil servants report use of statewide clipping services. Legislators, as we have seen, feel the need to keep firmly in touch with their local press. Hence in the New York City area, while all read or see their weeklies, they also mention the *New York Daily News* and the *New York Post*. On Long Island there is *Newsday*, widely mentioned for its investigative successes. Upstate the local daily or dailies are consumed with close attention by all legislators. Nearly one-quarter of the civil servants read newspapers from other upstate cities, while nearly 10 percent saw the *Wall Street Journal* regularly. Generally speaking, legislators seem to see *more* newspapers than civil servants, but the geographic spread and so-called quality of their reading is not greater. Moreover, the Albany papers and the *New York Times* provide a common ground of daily reading during the session of the Legislature and, for legislative leaders, year-round.[c]

How do these readers assess the coverage of State politics and government in the newspapers they read? Clearly, both groups read their newspapers for more than their professional concerns, but both groups did rank those concerns as dominant in their choice of reading. First, then, what did they think of the volume of coverage? Here civil servants were slightly more satisfied than legislators, more than 40 percent of whom claimed to be dissatisfied with this aspect.[d] One New York City Democrat claimed, "TV is worse than print—they never probe," and added that "if state papers were like Albany papers in type and volume of cover, it [the Legislature] would be much more responsive." A civil servant pointed to "grossly inadequate cover of the management of State government . . . woeful ignorance on the alternatives that might have been chosen in making different budgetary decisions." The differences may be explicable in terms of what is read; more civil servants rely on the heavily State-government-oriented Albany newspapers than do legislators. Neither group, anyway, is very satisfied—about 5 percent in each case—and this attitude is exemplified in the four-fifths of each group subscribing to the view that there were areas of State political and governmental activity that "need publicity and don't get it." A New York City Republican said resentfully, "City Hall is big news for the City papers, but we're more significant for the people." A downstate suburban Democrat noted that the press "looks at the Governor's budget proposal and at the final result—it ignores the middle period when the Legislature gets down to it." A civil servant observed, "New York State is not getting the government it is paying for," while another observed the reluctance of agencies to publicize achievements in case these were "converted to a political issue and torn apart by special interests." Given these attitudes, the fact that 58 percent of the legislators and 62 percent of the civil servants expressed themselves as satisfied with the volume of coverage in the press is less impressive. Interview experience suggests that it was a sometimes weary, and often reluctant, expression of the viewpoint, "What can one do?"

An analysis of the party component in these figures suggests part of the explanation. Democrats were twice as dissatisfied with the volume of coverage as were Republicans, and Liberals were 50 percent more dissatisfied than Conservatives. More than Republicans and Conservatives, both groups were concerned to stress the "ignored" areas of State government. Almost certainly this is a direct comment on the New York City daily press and its State-level coverage—the feast-or-famine tendencies that many legislators noted. More generally, it is a reflection on the low salience of State politics and on pressure from local and international news in what, after all, are *primarily* regional (if not national) newspapers that circulate in New York State. Legislators and civil servants know this, but still question the priorities of editorial staffs in adopting the mix of news that they do.

Volume of coverage is one thing, while accuracy, comprehension, and distortion are quite other features that these special publics are vitally interested in. First, what are their attitudes about accuracy and comprehension? Here the effort was made to get some idea of how journalists were evaluated purely on such technical matters as understanding briefings, getting quotations correct, and so forth. On the whole the feeling was that journalists do pass these important tests. A leading Republican summed up this feeling by saying, "Given the limits of the press, the effort is made." Nevertheless, 16 percent of legislators and over one-fifth of civil servants fault reporters in this respect. Democrats and Republicans seem equally dubious.[e] Liberals alone—perhaps generalizing from the *New York Times*—seemed ready to give the press high marks for accuracy. A downstate Republican recalled, "One member carries a golf bag in here and so we all do so, according to the press." A New York City Democrat asserted that "they're never quite accurate—a good story is not a true story." More seriously, a New York City Republican mentioned a case in which words were attributed to him even though he had not met the reporter. When challenged, the reporter said, "If I had called, you would have said it."

Civil service responses are more heavily qualified, since as many say they have "mixed" opinions as have favorable ones. More serious is the point that three-fifths of them—and four-fifths of legislators—claim that sometimes they personally gave or witnessed a briefing of a journalist and noted afterward how the published report "was still filled with inaccuracies." None of the groups saw this as a frequent occurrence, but, equally, none saw it as rare. Republicans and Conservatives were marginally less likely to claim any experience of it.[f] While the frequency varied, legislators and civil servants clearly accepted the phenomenon as a fact of life. It was yet another reason for a New York City Democrat to say, "That's why we are told all the time that the press is the enemy."

What about the readability and presentation of political news from the State level? Civil servants, who expressed the most qualified remarks on journalistic accuracy, were more ready than legislators to express satisfaction—but only as prelude to sometimes scathing criticism. Readability, to these individuals, was achieved at the expense of accuracy: the charge, in short, of sensationalizing. As one put it, "They attempt to generate reader interest by overkill." Another added that the media desire to make news, and this usually "translates to criticism." An upstate Democrat noted that "reporters are the voice of their editors—for them all is bad in government." Legislators, who were quick to claim inaccuracies, were quick also to affirm that State politics was not made readable. Only 40 percent expressed themselves as satisfied on this score—Republicans being slightly more critical than Democrats.[g] Legislators, like journalists, have to engage public interest, and their task—as they see it—is made more difficult by sensational and ill-informed intrusions by the press.

Legislators, of course, may be partisan in their appreciation—or journalists and editors may be partisan in their reporting. Is this the connection between the responses? Certainly journalistic errors are not put down to difficulties of access to news, since all legislators and 85 percent of civil servants believe that journalists have enough access to news in the State; indeed, "too much" was a frequent response.[h] Nor can the explanation lie simply in the overall competence of journalists to make use of the facilities open to them. Civil servants, by a majority of 55 percent, were prepared to accept the ability and willingness of news writers to use such facilities, though most of them claimed to detect some of the Albany press corps as too prone to rely on press releases. Legislators were just as qualified in their responses; 39 percent expressed confidence, and 42 percent reported a "mixed" reaction.[i] Nearly three-quarters of them saw too much "press release dependency" in some quarters, Republicans and Conservatives being much more frequent critics of journalistic competence and gullibility—"government by press release," as one scornfully dismissed it.[j]

There is, clearly, a marked lack of agreement on journalistic performance. Access is not regarded as a problem, but zeal or ability is in certain cases. Might such a disagreement over performance be attributable to perceptions of bias in news handling? Legislators and civil servants were asked whether in the coverage and handling of political news—*as opposed to explicit editorializing*—they detected discernible bias. Few legislators seemed in doubt, only 6 percent seeing no bias, 66 percent seeing bias, and 25 percent reporting a mixed situation.[k] A downstate suburban Republican claimed to see no bias "except to the sensational," whereas another of similar political complexion said flatly that he saw "very definite bias from the fifties onward; government by the Fourth Estate." Civil servants seemed much more divided: 38 percent perceived no bias, 43 percent claimed to see it, while a further 14 percent reported a mixed situation. One noted, not entirely jovially, that the "*Times* has a position on everything, and it is embedded in concrete." Another said bluntly, "All news is biased, depending on who writes it." It is immediately acknowledged, of course, that even to raise the question of bias serves to predispose some respondents to harden their feelings into a position or even to confess feelings and views they may hold only on occasion and with little conviction. The positions taken may gain in credibility, however, if the nature of the supposed bias is explored and its origins examined.

First, then, what is called bias for these groups? It seems not to be the distortion of news that is printed so much as the disregard of certain news and the overconcentration of attention on some individuals, departments, or agencies; Democrats and Liberals especially claimed to notice this. True, one-fifth of the Legislative mentions and one-tenth of the civil servants' mentions pointed to actual distortion. But both groups (Legislators, 70 percent, and civil servants, over 80 percent of mentions) lean much more toward the assertion of a silence on certain news areas or of either a mistaken concentration on, for example, the Governor (for legislators), or the harassment of a department (for civil servants).[l] "They miss many significant issues" said one respondent, and another cited the Department of Mental Hygiene as an example for which "the percentage of news time devoted to slanted harassment would be about 90%." Each group, in fact, had clear ideas on what it meant by bias.

Second, why is there bias? Civil service responses were careful. A fifth mentioned political partisanship and nearly a third cited publisher or editor attitudes. One quoted with relish the old jibe against the *New York Times*—"All the news that fitted we print." A few (12 percent) claimed to see hostility to government institutions themselves. More (18 percent) were ready to blame journalists, one noting that "Any bias stems more from ignorance or the emotion of creating a sensational story." By contrast, Legislators were much clearer, nearly a half blaming journalists. Only 6 percent saw editors or journalists as surrogates for voters. Reporters, for these lawmakers, were as much employees of their editors as the editors were in turn employees of their publishers. Claimed one grumpy New York City Democrat, "Nixon was right to note that the press got lost in its own ability . . . they felt they could do a better job than us." A Liberal New York City Democrat said, "They undervalue their effectiveness and what they do and, also, what we do." An upstate Republican commented scathingly on another aspect, namely, the press as business: "Why, they'll attack City Hall just to raise their income from Public Notices." And another leading Republican noted that the press "panders to people's emotions rather than the other characteristics they might have; the better ones [journalists] feel the need to express themselves and feel creative . . . in their reporting."ᵐ

More than half the Legislators and civil servants agreed that the mass media had serious faults when it came to being vehicles for politically informing the public. Legislators, more than civil servants, were likely to mention that newspapers compressed political news to fit their essentially commercial orientation (28 percent and 5 percent, respectively), and among Legislators Democrats and Liberals were more ready than Republicans and Conservatives to say this. Civil servants were three times as likely as Legislators to be concerned about the press's giving the public an inaccurate factual base from which to comprehend and evaluate government. Usually, when Legislators criticized journalists for their criteria of newsworthiness, the Legislators' own views and concerns were not being covered. A critical civil servant was likely to have in mind the media's overconcentration on the Governor and Legislature and lack of attention to important State agencies. Such civil servants reflected that in the much expanded State governmental apparatus a governor's or a legislator's capacity to make more than marginal change was *very* limited, yet the media concentrated too much on such actors.[n]

The predominance of this motif and the perceived independence of the press from Legislature and civil service is noteworthy. It is, moreover, testified to by attitudes elicited in answers to other questions on press-government relations. The fear of the press and the need for great care in dealing with it are evident in the almost shocked, near-total rejection by both groups of the proposition that it might be good policy to issue vague or half-baked press releases; "They would kill us," said one legislator.[o] One or two others were less fearful of misleading the media. "Sure," said a New York City Democrat, "my staff *help* reporters to find things out"; and another Democrat (from upstate) commented on colleagues' "playing the game—some do since they like the show game." Such a healthy respect, though evinced generally, need not necessarily preclude too much managing of the press by certain leading legislators and their staffs. One-fifth of the civil servants and one-third of the legislators agreed with the claim of a critic that the press was in danger of some degree of co-optation by legislators. Almost certainly, there was a clear distinction along partisan lines being made by these legislators. Roughly equal proportions of all groups thought there was co-optation at times. Democrats and especially Liberals were inclined to allude to the situation under Rockefeller in their responses, while Republicans and Conservatives referred to the present.[p] Thinking about the charge of co-optation, a jaundiced civil servant noted, "Every newsman wants a state job but they [the Legislature] don't do better than we do." A skeptical New York City Republican put any possibility of co-optation down to the simple proposition that "journalists are lazy."

The closeness, if it exists, was not seen as existing on conditions set wholly by legislators, even less by civil servants. Asked bluntly, "What do you have to do to get into the columns of the *New York*

Times?'' both groups testified to the power and independence of that newspaper. Three-quarters of the civil servants and nearly 60 percent of the legislators mentioned that they would have to be involved on an issue that the newspaper itself defined as important; Republicans and Conservatives seemed more certain of this than did Democrats and Liberals. One civil servant mentioned only, ''use good P.R.''; and, interestingly, to judge by his responses, he would be a political liberal. One-eighth of legislators—all Democrats and Liberals—mentioned that it ''depends on where you're from,'' an allusion to the perceived New York City orientation of the *New York Times*. A New York City Democrat took care to be precise in his answer: ''Those who get in live in Manhattan and share its orientation.''[q] A civil servant, reflecting on his earlier days in education, noted that the *New York Times* would tend to cover that field, ''since in New York State education is more important than organized religion.'' In general, interview experience suggests that the major dailies of the State as well as the *New York Times* are seen as an independent and, on occasion, very potent third party in a series of relationships with the Legislature and the executive. As such, it is necessary, particularly for legislators, to try very hard for frictionless relationships with both their local newspapers and, more broadly, the press corps.

Claiming a good relationship with the media was almost reflex for legislators—some four-fifths did so—while only *one* (a Liberal Democrat) admitted to a poor relationship.[r] Interview experience suggests strongly that in very many cases, as seen by legislators, this was a relationship preserved only by stoic endurance on their part. Many of the claims to good relations were made wearily, and some seemed to come through gritted teeth. On his press relations one upstate Democrat noted, ''Friendly enough—but I'm wary,'' while a leading upstate Republican remarked that his relations were ''selectively good. . . . I'm not the newsworthy type.'' Civil servants generally have a more distant and intermittent relationship with the media. Only one claimed to have no relationship at all with news writers, and three admitted to a poor relationship. The remainder claimed at least a fairly good relationship (63 percent)—''a correct relationship,'' as one commented rather primly.

The question of correctness is no mere academic point. In the atmosphere of continuing revelations of national government manipulation of the media and of supposed previous journalistic docility, as sunshine laws are being enacted and greater control of lobbying is being considered, propriety in relationships is now honored less in the breach. As there exists a necessity to claim good relations with the media, so, too, questions on the propriety of news of public officials or journalistic decency and trustworthiness are likely to produce careful answers for public consumption.

Only one civil servant, but one-fifth of the legislators believed in an absolute public right to know *anything* about public officials, elective or appointed. The most frequent reply (95 percent from civil servants and 81 percent from legislators) was that disclosure in such cases should always be job related and that as far as possible the family and friends of public officials had a right to privacy in face of harassment and prying. In a question aimed at clarifying *emphasis* among Legislators, Republicans and Conservatives were clearly more concerned than Democrats or Liberals to stress the restraints on any right to know.[5] Summing up for many, a New York City Democrat expostulated, "There is no such constitutional thing as an absolute right to know—there *is* a right to sell papers." A suburban Democrat noted, "We are not public figures twenty-four hours a day. . . . familiarity breeds contempt." A civil servant remarked tartly that the media relay personal stories that "would ordinarily not be printed if the principals were business people who pay for advertising."

Such responses, of course, do not go very far to meet the dilemma for journalists—faced day by day—of what exactly is or *might be* job related about public officials. Whether journalists in the State satisfied legislators or civil servants on this score was probed. Asked whether journalists usually accepted a need for a *degree* of government confidentiality and personal decency in their coverage, over two-thirds of each group unequivocally answered yes to both questions. On both, however, the dissenting minorities among legislators were not insignificant. Twenty-nine percent felt that journalists did not accept the need for any confidentiality, and 32 percent felt the same on the question of personal decency. The minorities among Democrats and Liberals were considerably larger than among Republicans and Conservatives.[1] The reasons for this are no doubt complicated, but among journalists, for example, they would in part be put down to the much more guarded posture of Republicans toward the press. One senior suburban Republican complained bitterly of what he called a double standard of morality: "If a committee chairman is entertained by clients of his committee, that is very bad. If he is whoring, drinking, and incapable of doing his job, that is less bad." Another Republican complained of finding it impossible to see where the media "draw their line," and yet another said flatly of newspapers, "They shouldn't be scandal sheets."

As on many occasions earlier noted, the civil service response was less forthright, a majority either being reluctant to answer or claiming to have a "mixed" opinion on both counts. "We have asked them to wait a month on a story," wrote one on the point of confidentiality, but then added significantly, "we pick them carefully."

Having now looked at a variety of legislative and bureaucratic attitudes toward the media, we have seen that both groups are well informed on the news game and are exposed to a variety of newspapers. It is clear, however, that the *New York Times* (year-around) and the Albany newspapers (during the session) are more influential than other newspapers and that none escaped the widespread unease among both groups over what is seen as their too frequent inaccuracies in news reporting. Four-fifths of both groups claim *personal* experience of actually witnessing such inaccuracies. Further, legislators and civil servants detect bias of one sort or another in media, especially press, news reporting. They seem ready to blame editorial policies of newspapers and radio/television stations certainly, but journalists even more. Finally, both groups claim that such bias has increased in the post-Watergate era.

This is a fairly severe indictment. Before the truth of it can be assessed, however, other witnesses—namely, the press corps who produce that news—must be examined. How does the working journalist in Albany meet the world of State government and politics? Bias for one individual, after all, may be necessity —or truth —for another.

DATA

Figures in parentheses	= n
All others	= %
Party Affiliation	Legislators only

a. In your district how many newspapers are there? Television/radio stations?

	Newspapers			TV/radio stations	
	0-5	6-10	11+	0-5	6-10
Legislators	14.3 (4)	42.9 (12)	42.9 (12)	39.3 (11)	60.7 (17)

b. Is it easier to get on with your own local reporters or with those at the capitol?

	Local		REASONS		
	Yes	No	Familiarity	Local focus	Statewide focus
Legislators	77.4 (24)	22.6 (7)	22.2 (6)	70.4 (19)	7.4 (2)

c. What newspapers do you read regularly? [Mentions]

	NY Times	NY Daily News	NY Post	Albany	My Locals	Clipping service	Others
REGULARLY							
Legislators	27.8 (23)	18.1 (15)	9.6 (8)	9.6 (8)	16.9 (14)	8.4 (7)	9.6 (8)
C. Servants	35.6 (16)	8.9 (4)		37.8 (17)	6.7 (3)		11.1 (5)
OCCASIONALLY							
Legislators	8.1 (3)	8.1 (3)	10.8 (4)	51.4 (19)	8.1 (3)	5.4 (2)	8.1 (3)
C. Servants	35.7 (5)	14.3 (2)	7.1 (1)	14.2 (2)		14.2 (2)	14.2 (2)

d. Are you satisfied with the volume of State political news reported?

	Very satisfied	Satisfied	Dissatisfied	Very dissatisfied
Legislators	6.5 (2)	51.6 (16)	38.7 (12)	3.2 (1)
C. Servants	4.8 (1)	57.1 (12)	38.1 (8)	
Democrats	6.3 (1)	31.2 (5)	56.3 (9)	6.3 (1)
Republicans	6.7 (1)	73.3 (11)	20.0 (3)	
Liberals	11.1 (1)	33.3 (3)	44.4 (4)	11.1 (1)
Conservatives		70.0 (7)	30.0 (3)	

e. Generally speaking, would you say that political news is accurately reported in NYS?

	Yes	No	Mixed	DK
Legislators	48.4 (15)	16.1 (5)	35.5 (11)	
C. Servants	38.1 (8)	23.8 (5)	38.1 (8)	
Democrats	50.0 (8)	18.8 (3)	31.3 (5)	
Republicans	46.7 (7)	13.3 (2)	40.0 (6)	
Liberals	75.0 (6)		25.0 (2)	
Conservatives	50.0 (4)	25.0 (2)	25.0 (2)	

f. If not, can you think of a case when you personally gave or witnessed *either* a background *or* a public briefing of a journalist—and noted afterward how his/her reporting was still filled with inaccuracies?

	Often	Sometimes	Never
Legislators	10.0 (3)	76.7 (23)	13.3 (4)
C. Servants	23.5 (4)	58.8 (10)	17.6 (3)
Democrats	6.3 (1)	87.5 (14)	6.3 (1)
Republicans	14.3 (2)	64.3 (9)	21.4 (3)
Liberals	11.1 (1)	77.8 (7)	11.1 (1)
Conservatives	10.0 (1)	70.0 (7)	20.0 (2)

g. Are you satisfied, generally speaking, with the *way* political news is reported—presentation, readability, etc.?

	Very satisfied	Satisfied	Dissatisfied	Very dissatisfied	Mixed
Legislators		39.4 (13)	45.5 (15)	6.0 (2)	9.1 (3)
C. Servants		52.4 (11)	42.9 (9)		4.8 (1)
Democrats		43.8 (7)	43.8 (7)	12.5 (2)	
Republicans		40.0 (6)	53.3 (8)	6.7 (1)	
Liberals		33.3 (3)	44.4 (4)	22.2 (2)	
Conservatives		40.0 (4)	60.0 (6)		

h. Do you think, in general, journalists are given enough access to information (news) and newsmakers in NYS?

	Yes	No	Mixed
Legislators	100.0 (31)		
C. Servants	85.0 (17)	5.0 (1)	10.0 (2)
Democrats	100.0 (16)		
Republicans	100.0 (15)		
Liberals	100.0 (9)		
Conservatives	100.0 (10)		

i. Generally speaking, is it your impression that journalists are able and willing to make use of the news facilities open to them?

	Yes	No	Mixed
Legislators	38.7 (12)	19.4 (6)	41.9 (13)
C. Servants	54.5 (12)	13.6 (3)	31.8 (7)
Democrats	43.8 (7)	12.5 (2)	43.8 (7)
Republicans	33.3 (5)	26.7 (4)	40.0 (6)
Liberals	33.3 (3)	11.1 (1)	55.6 (5)
Conservatives	40.0 (4)	40.0 (4)	20.0 (2)

j. Do journalists depend on press releases too much?

	Too many	Some	None	DK
Legislators	16.7 (5)	56.7 (17)	20.0 (6)	6.6 (2)
C. Servants	5.0 (1)	65.0 (13)	20.0 (4)	10.0 (2)

k. In you own experience, and speaking generally, for the coverage and handling of news—*as opposed to explicit editorializing* in NYS—would you say there is/is not discernible bias in the handling of political news?

	Yes	No	Mixed	DK
Legislators	65.6 (21)	6.3 (2)	25.0 (8)	3.1 (1)
C. Servants	42.8 (9)	38.0 (8)	14.3 (3)	4.7 (1)
Democrats	76.5 (13)	5.8 (1)	17.6 (3)	
Republicans	53.0 (8)	6.7 (1)	33.3 (5)	6.7 (1)
Liberals	88.9 (8)		11.1 (1)	
Conservatives	40.0 (4)		50.0 (5)	10.0 (1)

l. If yes, is this in the form of (1) disregarding news; (2) overconcentrating on some, as opposed to other, individuals; (3) harassing certain departments by *only* unfavorable publicity; (4) distorting of stories; (5) other? [Mentions]

	1	2	3	4	5
Legislators	35.0 (14)	35.0 (14)	5.0 (2)	20.0 (8)	5.0 (2)
C. Servants	30.3 (10)	21.2 (7)	27.3 (9)	9.0 (3)	12.1 (4)
Democrats	39.1 (9)	43.5 (10)	8.7 (2)	8.7 (2)	
Republicans	29.4 (5)	23.5 (4)		35.3 (6)	11.8 (2)
Liberals	38.5 (5)	5.4 (7)	7.7 (1)		7.7 (1)
Conservatives	23.1 (3)	23.1 (3)	7.7 (1)	38.5 (5)	7.7 (1)

m. If so, what are the origins of these biases? [Mentions]

	Party politics	Hostility to government operations	Hostility to government institutions	Reporter ideology	Popular attitudes	Publisher/editor attitudes
Legislators	8.0 (4)	2.0 (1)	2.0 (1)	46.0 (23)	6.0 (3)	36.0 (18)
C. Servants	20.6 (7)	8.8 (3)	11.8 (4)	17.6 (6)	11.8 (4)	29.4 (10)
Democrats	10.3 (3)	3.4 (1)	3.4 (1)	41.4 (12)	6.9 (2)	34.5 (10)
Republicans	4.8 (1)			52.4 (11)	4.8 (1)	38.1 (8)
Liberals	6.2 (1)			43.8 (7)	6.2 (1)	43.8 (7)
Conservatives				46.7 (7)		53.3 (8)

n. Is it implicit in the news-gathering process? If so, what do you mean? [Mentions]

(1) Newspapers basically are media for commerical news—other news is squeezed by that and sports, ads, etc.;

(2) Newspapers are fearful of getting involved in politics—their editorializing and coverage is "phony," participation;

(3) Newspapers give a distorted view of the world of politics and certainly of government—an inaccurate factual base to evaluate politics;

(4) Newspapers and journalists, with their criteria of newsworthiness, cannot be expected adequately to keep up public political education;

(5) Class or local bias;

(6) No.

	1	2	3	4	5	6
Legislators	27.5 (11)	2.5 (1)	7.5 (3)	60.0 (24)	2.5 (1)	
C. Servants	4.8 (1)	4.8 (1)	23.8 (5)	52.4 (11)	9.5 (2)	4.8 (1)
Democrats	34.8 (8)	4.3 (1)	8.7 (2)	47.8 (11)	4.3 (1)	
Republicans	17.6 (3)		5.9 (1)	76.5 (13)		
Liberals	38.5 (5)		7.7 (1)	53.8 (7)		
Conservatives	28.6 (4)	7.1 (1)	7.1 (1)	57.1 (8)		

o. Do you think it is good policy to try to influence political news coverage by releasing vague or contradictory press releases?

	Often	Sometimes	Never	DK
Legislators	3.2 (1)	9.7 (3)	87.1 (27)	
C. Servants		23.8 (5)	71.4 (15)	4.8 (1)

p. Would you agree with a recent writer who claimed that the NYS press was in danger of being co-opted by legislators and their staffs?

	Yes	No	Some	DK
Legislators		65.6 (21)	31.3 (10)	3.2 (1)
C. Servants		71.4 (15)	19.0 (4)	9.5 (2)
Democrats		70.6 (12)	29.4 (5)	
Republicans		60.0 (9)	33.3 (5)	6.7 (1)
Liberals		62.5 (5)	37.5 (3)	
Conservatives		60.0 (6)	30.0 (3)	10.0 (1)

q. What do you have to do to get into the columns of the New York Times? [Mentions]

	Be involved in issues	Support debates it favors	Be anti-leadership	Be outrageous	Be from NYC	Use P.R.	DK
Legislators	43.8 (14)	12.5 (4)	6.3 (2)	15.6 (5)	12.5 (4)		9.4 (3)
C. Servants	75.0 (15)			5.0 (1)	5.0 (1)	5.0 (1)	10.0 (2)
Democrats	37.5 (6)	6.3 (1)	6.3 (1)	12.5 (2)	25.0 (4)		12.5 (2)
Republicans	53.3 (8)	20.0 (3)	6.7 (1)	20.0 (3)			
Liberals	44.4 (4)			11.1 (1)	33.3 (3)		11.1 (1)
Conservatives	50.0 (5)	30.0 (3)	10.0 (1)	10.0 (1)			

r. How would you characterize your relations with the press?

	Very good	Good	Fairly good	Poor	Nonexistent
Legislators	12.9 (4)	64.5 (20)	19.3 (6)	3.2 (1)	
C. Servants	26.3 (5)	36.8 (7)	15.8 (3)	15.8 (3)	5.3 (1)
Democrats	6.3 (1)	62.5 (10)	25.0 (4)	6.3 (1)	
Republicans	20.0 (3)	66.7 (10)	13.3 (2)		
Liberals	11.1 (1)	66.7 (6)	11.1 (1)	11.1 (1)	
Conservatives		70.0 (7)	30.0 (3)		

s. Are there restraints on the public's "right to know" about public officials?

	No	No, except if news not job related	Yes, unless job related
Legislators	19.4 (6)	51.6 (16)	29.0 (9)
C. Servants	4.7 (1)	47.6 (10)	47.6 (10)
Democrats	18.8 (3)	62.5 (10)	18.8 (3)
Republicans	25.0 (3)	40.0 (6)	40.0 (6)
Liberals	22.2 (2)	66.7 (6)	11.1 (1)
Conservatives	10.0 (1)	60.0 (6)	30.0 (3)

t. Do you think journalists, generally, accept the need for a degree of government secrecy and personal decency in their job?

	SECRECY				DECENCY			
	Yes	No	Mixed	DK	Yes	No	Mixed	DK
Legislators	67.7 (21)	29.0 (9)	3.2 (1)		67.7 (21)	32.2 (10)		
C. Servants	71.4 (15)	9.5 (2)	14.3 (3)	4.8 (1)	75.0 (15)	5.0 (1)	10.0 (2)	10.0 (2)

7

The View from the Press Room—The Capitol Press Corps

Legislators and civil servants show a moderately high degree of consensus on the competence and impartiality of the Albany press corps. They are, after all, observers of the media over a period of between five and twenty-five years; they *do* have some inside knowledge of the journalists' task; and none appeared to have any personal animus against them. Separately and together they constitute a vitally important public for political journalism in New York State, one whose views journalists themselves are professionally concerned to note. Do they—can they—know what it is like to be a member of the Albany press corps? Do they know what it is like to be a working journalist in Albany or, indeed, how their own performance is measured by such a journalist? We have seen that legislators and civil servants view journalists with considerable caution and, at times, some ill-concealed resentment and even disdain. It is as well to view the behavior of journalists in part, as a reaction to this caution and occasional hostility. More than this, however, their behavior and attitudes are products of their whole situation—both generally as members of the Albany press corps and particularly as newspaper X's staff at Albany.

What was that situation? To begin with, how accessible were newsmakers to them; how legitimate a place were they accorded in the scheme of things? Formally, at least, the situation seemed highly favorable—the press quarters were provided *free* by the State in the capitol. From the Governor on down, through the department and agency heads and the leadership in the Legislature, there appeared to be no lack of press secretaries, aides, and so on. No department or agency seemed complete without its public information office, usually staffed by ex-journalists who were well paid by comparison with the reporters whom they were there, in part, to serve. No one, as reporters noted, could accuse the government of New York State of being anything other than zealous for the information flow to the public, and the trend was toward ever more information.

Some legislators and civil servants felt that the government was too open. Do journalists agree? Not surprisingly, they do not, though three-quarters of them subscribed to the view that New York government and politics was "adequately accessible" to journalists.[a] Although generally in agreement with this opinion, one senior journalist noted how both the "legislature and executive need a crash course. . . . they must understand the role of media. There is a lack of understanding of what this business is all about." Another journalist noted that the civil servants "see their P.R. people as protection from the press." Many had various suggestions for improvements in access, which will be discussed later. For the moment it is sufficient to note that four-fifths of the journalists considered political news as easy or very easy to secure, though some of them made the point that the "why" behind the political news was much less easy to secure were than the facts as such.[b] The latter are easily gained in press conferences, press releases, debates, interviews, and the like.

For the working journalist the facts are but a prelude to the follow-up on a story by personal contacts, which, for most of them, reveal the real news story. "Knowing what question to ask," said one, "is *the* problem when the government is so big." A veteran journalist agreed, noting that "we break more stories than New York City—second only to Washington. Our governors are presidential material, our state innovates, hence we have masses of news." Believing as they do that public statements almost always have a component of careful silence or half-truth, they see one of their most important tasks as the digging out of the story behind the story and the highlighting of this for the public. Digging may be too strong a word, since many journalists find themselves the routine target of a great deal of "off the record" information designed to put somebody—usually a staff member's legislative or agency boss—"on the record" on some question or other. The story that a good journalist may quickly build up mentally is a product more often of collating deliberate leaks than of digging as such. It is this routinized reconstruction that allows nearly half of the journalists to claim that more than 70 percent of their political news derives from their own investigation.[c] In their own eyes, they are in Albany, not for uncovering facts—"let the wires [wire services] have them"—but for alerting editors and publishers and then the public to what is "really" at stake, what may become tomorrow's "facts."

This attitude gives more depth to their recognition that the system is adequately accessible. It is not really the formal accessibility that they have in mind so much as their personal capacity to exploit actors' willingness to talk off the record. Formal accessibility is not as valuable to them as is a fragmented, rivalry-prone structure of government and a great many competing ambitions and personalities. Currently, for example, the divided party control of the Legislature, the succession problem among Republicans, and the series of major revenue crises have together provided journalists with endless so-called leaks, as partisans of one sort or another signal each other in the media and strive for advantage.

Indeed, New York State government and politics may be too accessible nowadays in the sense that too much news is a severe constraint in itself, so far as journalists are concerned. Quite simply, it is not only that too many good stories may jostle each other on one or two days; but a large and complex governmental structure is too much for one or two reporters to cover under more normal circumstances. For example, in 1975, when a new administration took office and scores of senior jobs had to be filled, and in 1976 when hard policy choices had to be made for New York, then the task became well-nigh impossible even though the press corps was reinforced by extra journalists who came only for the session.

The constraint of too much news must be set in the context of other routine constraints seen by journalists. Four-fifths of them see legal considerations—principally libel—as rarely or never a constraint on them, if only, as many put it, because "we know the score so well." The fear has become an internalized constraint—part of job socialization—but is real enough for all that. Certainly in the current "investigative" atmosphere journalists may find themselves skirting legality more often—and more willingly. But what of other constraints? Those of newspaper space and deadlines are, again, part of the job and its attendant behavior. The resident Albany correspondent usually comes with or secures promises of a given space from his or her editor. Yet despite these assurances —and socialization into the job—some 40 percent or so of journalists noted that considerations of space in their newspapers and deadlines for stories were always a constraint. Many reporters complained of "controversial late night votes" and recalled that Rockefeller saw to it that "big bills came on early in the day." As described earlier, a Legislature that does not meet daily, that usually convenes around lunchtime on Monday and Wednesday, and that often becomes snarled in procedural or minor matters is a potential nightmare even for the reporter on the morning daily. The journalist representing an evening newspaper is, as one put it, often forced to guess by 10 A.M. what news is likely to break in a committee or in a full session that afternoon. The result is a much heavier reliance on the more oblique, more analytic, less fact-bound piece that nevertheless, stands a chance of being upstaged by events. So, too, does television, which covers little because the networks have now withdrawn their reporters from Albany. Public television now has its statewide weekly program, which goes out on Thursdays —the end of the week for legislature—and is repeated later. Yet two-thirds of the journalists believe television is given more ready access and, because it does so little analysis, is more manipulable by politicians than is the print press.

Again, if by real accessibility journalists mean leaks of all sorts, how great a constraint is source protection? In Watergate fashion, does New York State have its "plumbers" whose task is to track down and plug leaks? Journalists, of course, would reply that the public good is usually served by leaks and that they themselves become connoisseurs of the phenomenon. A "blown source" is no good at all to them, and they strive to avoid such an offense to journalistic ethics. New York State has a large, fragmented government, and few leaks, it would seem, could come from *only* one source. Yet nearly one-third (30 percent) of them reported source protection as a frequent constraint and a further 43 percent noted it as occasional.[d] Frequency of occurrence may be less significant for journalists than the question of which story or type of story is castrated by the need to preserve confidentiality. As one commented, "Normally, if the story is easily traceable, you're not going to get it [the leak] in the first place." Another, agreeing, noted how "it is rare for us to learn anything that isn't intended by someone." So critical a forum is the *New York Times* considered that its reporters "get a lot handed to them—more at times than they can handle," remarked a reporter from elsewhere. The Governor and legislators were pictured as working always "with the *Times* [news] cycle in mind." The agencies, like Rockefeller, have no news available on Fridays and reporters see news being held for the Sunday newspapers, especially again the *New York Times*.

Overall, anyway, source protection is not the main constraint. Without a doubt, for journalists it is the lack of personnel.[e] Most of the newspapers have one, or at most two, reporters in Albany on a regular basis. The "session men"—the reporters who come in to help during the session—are sometimes reporters who cover Albany from afar and have their own contacts in Albany and elsewhere. Equally, they can be people who have to rely on the regulars at Albany for contacts to develop stories. One journalist used the term "hit men" to describe them, since some of them, he said, "are here today, gone tomorrow, and come with the story written." A point worth noting is that this description is remarkably similar to that often used by nonjournalists to describe journalists in general. Some of the session men exemplify to their Albany-based colleagues the very vices they feel are inherent in their own situation—namely, inadequate time to research stories and, hence, too heavy a reliance on received wisdom or loose speculation masquerading as "think" pieces. The old gibe that much foreign news comes from one colleague interviewing another in some foreign bar (or worse, in a bar near the newspaper's home office) contains more than a germ of truth for serious journalists.

Many Albany reporters would agree that something of the kind could be said of Albany news, and they are in no doubt about the cause: too much happening, too quickly, too covertly in a huge governmental structure, for too few reporters to cover. A veteran reporter noted that "we're more dependent on handouts than we ever were—there is little manpower to check releases." Another, commenting on the difficulties of explaining the significance of news, stated, "to get the story in perspective takes time, and we haven't got it too often." A disenchanted colleague said bluntly, "Editors will wait three or four days [for a story involving research] and no more." The lack of personnel and the competitive ethic of journalists means that integrity can easily suffer. Said a veteran, "Albany is no exception to the rule that quick but poor-quality guys can go far." Fully 70 percent of those questioned cited personnel (or time, which is the same thing) as the constraint of constraints—four times as many, for example, as mentioned protection of sources, and nearly six times as many as mentioned space considerations.

Journalists in Albany see their situation as a difficult one. Inevitably, they cope with it in ways that give rise on occasion to difficulties with colleagues and sources. Some favor a resigned acceptance of traditional news sources and news areas. Others realize full well that in so doing—and all tend to have to—they are active participants and perpetrators of a style of politics and a scheme of values that they may disapprove of. Some reporters are heavily concerned with developing news, assuming an investigative or advocacy posture toward the State and its political and bureaucratic elite. Though they are often freed from the need to cover routine news, the usual constraints on news gathering still apply and are supplemented by others. Asked about constraints on investigative journalism, nearly one-half mentioned the need for more time and personnel. The other half, in their various choices, illuminated the whole scene. First, they said that New York State is a large and complex government (12 percent): "even if we had more reporters," said one, "there would still be the question of *where* to look and *what* to look for." Again, not all journalists feel that investigation is their proper role (9 percent), or that they are equipped to undertake it in a situation in which access is unsatisfactory (9 percent)."The leadership has such control," remarked one, "that they can really slow you down and make life difficult." Second, almost a half stressed that investigative journalism is expensive in both time and personnel (hence money) and may—a cardinal sin for editors—lead nowhere. Hence, editors and publishers are loath to allow expensive senior reporters to become involved (9 percent), especially when they think their readers have only slight interest (6 percent).[f] "We have to be apologetic for finding nothing," said one; and another added, "Life just won't go into *their* 600-word segments." One thought that the situation could be summed up thus, "Publishers like a day's story for a day's pay, and investigation just isn't like that."

Investigative journalism must be seen in this context. It must also be set against editorial perception of the significance of State news. Nearly four-fifths of the journalists thought that State news was overshadowed in the public mind by local and Washington news:[g] "People like to read about those they think they know, or know of." Almost as many believed that this was principally a product of editorial perceptions at the various papers. "State news is often dull, but is highly significant," claimed one reporter. "New York City forgets that state exists—the papers are aware mostly, but can't thrust it down people's throats there." Only three journalists believed that State news was intrinsically less interesting than other news to voters. Three others said bluntly that the situation was a product of the weak position of Albany reporters on their newspapers and of the quality in the past of journalists sent to the State Capitol.[h] "There is generational change here," said one reporter, "and the younger reporters think Albany is an important place and a real promotion for them." In general, the situation is felt to be improving, and 60 percent of the journalists claim to be satisfied with the volume of state news currently printed in their papers.[i] This contrasts fairly sharply with the attitudes of legislators and civil servants. Perhaps journalists are more aware of the news that State news has to compete with daily—or perhaps they have been socialized into expectations that are too low. The news situation of the main New York City papers, in particular the

New York Times, has already been discussed: State news from Albany has to compete to enter the columns of the single most prestigious paper in the United States.

News from Albany itself is a product of news competition, of journalistic selection and presentation, and, not least, of governmental news management. Journalists are sought after almost as much as they seek people out. The seeking out takes a variety of forms—hand-delivered press releases, letters, telephone calls, personal visits; the press room at the capitol is often as congested as a busy airport terminal. The staffs of the Governor and of legislative leaders are frequent callers. Most journalists identify legislative staffs as more assiduous callers, though not more successful, than a variety of people who come from the agencies. The principal inducement to take an interest for journalists is certainly not the free lunch, but what they label as favoritism, namely, the attempt to give one or more journalists a scoop or a new angle on a story likely to break soon.[j] "I've never been offered a bribe," said one veteran, "but I get a lot of 'buddy-buddy' phone calls. The touchiness here is such that politicians keep clear and let their staffs try to be friendly." A colleague summed up the dilemma of those who see themselves needing to be highly informed, but uninvolved: "You can't be distant and expect to know what's going on."

The *New York Times* is the acknowledged target for the most assiduous cultivation by the political leadership and by groups outside the legislature. Its reporters and those of the wire services in Albany are regarded as bellwethers for the current lead story. Indeed, *New York Times* and *Newsday* reporters have been accused of creating their own agenda for the Legislature in 1975 and 1976 and sticking to it in terms of news coverage and editorial emphasis. There is, and perhaps has to be, a large element of pack journalism. One leading journalist said openly that he and a colleague consulted daily during the session to establish "what rubbish shall we avoid today?" This is a fair summation of the response of reporters to so-called news of bills that are not intended to pass, to "grandstanding" in committee and on the floor—to much, in short, that competition among reporters might lead them to cover, were it not for the pack leaders and the evolving, press-room consensus generated as the session proceeds.

In this context, are changes in party control likely to be a very significant variable in news production? Sixty percent of the journalists thought that the Democratic takeover of the governorship and the Assembly had made some difference in accessibility. Some put this down to what they saw as traditional Democratic "gabbiness." One noted that "the Republicans tend to see themselves as cautious gentlemen who do not wash dirty linen in public and [who] see the press as interlopers." More common was the view that Democrats, as the minority party for some years, had needed the press more and mistakenly assumed that journalists were their friends. Once they realized that "we are nobody's friends," as one newsman put it, then they would behave—journalists felt—not so much like Republicans as like "ins" instead of "outs."[k]

Party control might change, but whichever party dominated had to face a deluge of lobbying activity from outside groups. So, too, did journalists, who have been known quite often to leave the press room to avoid their lobbying. Over half of the news writers identified the various public interest groups as their most frequent visitors. "The 'goo goos' [good government groups] can be a nuisance," said one, "but they are an increasingly useful source of information." Business and labor lobbyists come much less frequently, and, as one claimed, "the real bad guys stay away from us and deal privately with legislators." The upsurge of good government groups in the State is congruent with the impact of generational change in the press room. Many of the reporters share sympathies with the spokespersons of such groups, though not, one newsman remarked, "their earnestness and occasional self-righteousness."[l]

What about the agencies? The greater distance between them and journalists was alluded to earlier. Much, if not most of their news, is neither as quickly nor as easily understood as that of the Legislature—nor as easily personalized. As seen by nine-tenths of the journalists, there is great variety in the degree of access accorded by agencies and this situation was ascribed by nearly three-quarters of them *not* to the substantive policy area of the agency, but to the attitudes of its top leadership.[m] "It depends on who is commissioner, and for how long he's been there," said one, while another stressed that "a new commissioner, seeking to impress the Governor, could be very cooperative.'' Each agency has its information office to assist both the press and the public. Nearly one-quarter of the journalists see their relations with those offices as unsatisfactory,[n] and even more claim to see the press releases of the agency as equally unsatisfactory. [o] "I understand their job," said one, "and it is not to be that helpful." A more critical newsman said of the public relations staff, "They are an apologetic group . . . who fear not for their agency but for themselves." More sympathetically, a newsman commented on the dilemma of information officers: "They can only say what they know is true, whereas we can put interpretations on what they say." The relationship clearly has mostly adversary qualities; about 70 percent of the journalists saw information staffs as employed, basically, to promote the agency by a "supply of favorable news."[p]

The question of legislative and agency public relations activity is instructive. Virtually all journalists report a degree of response to their stories—though, in Albany it is not a frequent occurrence. What is clear is that when it does occur (by visit, telephone, or letter), it is almost certain to come from a legislative or agency aide, a lobbyist, or an editor moved to act by one of these three groups. Agency feedback is the single most common source—nearly one-quarter of the instances cited coming from their public relations officers.[q] The public, by contrast, can seem to be very distant at times to journalists. Generally, it appears that newspapers forward to their Albany reporters only a small number of letters or telephone messages from the public. It is not surprising that reporters see themselves at times as in danger of writing for a small number of professional press consumers who know the reporters, read their work with great attention, are familiar with the detail of an issue and hence can correct a reporter on "fact," and, above all, are paid in effect *not* to ensure maximum public knowledge, but to protect the agency image. As one reporter noted, "thinly veiled hostility or resentment directed to oneself can be very wearing and its antithesis, friendly candor, very disarming." The customer for reporters is very close to them, and it may be hard to keep themselves from believing that the customer is mostly right. Some 68 percent of newswriters conceded that they "sometimes" anticipate feedback.[r] One respected reporter, for example, said he would not publish a critical piece on an agency without giving it prior warning. Another observed that even after years of experience, he could not predict what would really cause a stir: "You don't know when you're going to poke the nerve."

Journalists are well aware that they wield a potent weapon in their capacity to publicize and dramatize. In their own eyes, for the most part, they are confident that they work responsibly. Three-quarters of them denied acceptance of any absolute public right to know about public officials and their families and friends.[5] Where information clearly related to the performance of official duty, then publicity was in order. Where there was doubt, they should be cautious, take advice, seek more information, but—ultimately—be prejudiced in favor of printing, rather than not printing. One journalist waxed eloquent against printing grand jury leaks, an action he felt his profession was too prone to commit. "Currently it is the bad guys who are up—Nixon, etc.—but it could be the good guys, and they forget that." Generally, members of the press accepted the need for a degree of political and governmental secrecy—at least with regard to timing. Further, few of them had doubts that public officials were entitled to protection from malicious intent among journalists—40 percent, in fact, believed this protection could be be strengthened without loss of journalistic freedom.[t] Almost unanimously, journalists denied any wish to be political or personal peeping toms: "There *are* dangers in 'National Enquirerism,'" said one; and another added that "gossip must serve a function." To many reporters, however, there were more than a few people in the upper echelons of goverment who were ready to exploit journalistic restraint and who really did believe that freedom of the press meant favorable comment on themselves and silence, or unfair publicity, for their opponents.

One dissenter in the press room stood out. To him the press "played the game" with the polical elite too much already. If it was really doing the work of a free press, he argued, then it would soon unearth legislators and civil servants who were hostile to press freedom. So long as the proper sphere of politics was defined by politicians and of good administration by civil servants, and so long as political reporting ran in approved channels, then both groups easily overlooked the rare indiscretion or breach of confidence. He felt that "legislators and bureaucrats are comfortable with the press" and that any small signs of resentment at its behavior should never be taken as anything other than atypical: "Politicians have been given the benefit of the doubt for too long here, and elsewhere."

The contrast between these views and the mainstream is not as great as it might seem. Many journalists believe that their role, as surrogates for the voter, is to make and keep those in high places in government routinely uncomfortable. One of the ways the press does, or tries to do, this is by highlighting the gap between promise and performance and, further, by suggesting that the promises themselves were inadequate for the needs they sought to meet. This second role involves competing with the political elite to set out the items on the political agenda, a topic that we must return to later.

Journalists are only too well aware that covering State government and politics is fraught with difficulties. Sheer size and complexity of government, its potentiality for manipulating them, the pressure of the daily round—all contribute to a species of pack journalism that most reporters regret, but regard as inevitable. In their eyes, achieving adequacy of coverage—to say nothing of investigative journalism—is barely possible. Yet, there are changes in the attitudes of journalists and traumatic events in the State have long created a critical posture toward the gap between rhetoric and reality visible at many levels. Rockefeller's legacy has been a crisis that offers hope of influence to many members of the press.

Having now assessed the general attitudes of the three groups—legislators, civil servants, and journalists—toward each other, we may now go on to look at their *explicit* views on the press-government relationship. How do they see their interaction?

DATA

Figures in parentheses   = *n*
All others   = *%*

a. Generally, do you consider that State government in New York is adequately accessible to the media and, particularly, the press?

	Yes	*No*	*Mixed*
Journalists	72.7 (16)	27.3 (6)	

b. Generally speaking, how hard is access to political news?

	Very easy	*Easy*	*Hard*	*Very hard*	*DK*
Journalists	17.4 (4)	60.9 (14)	21.7 (5)		

c. What proportion of your political news would you say is derived from your own investigation and reconstruction?

	30% or less	*31-70%*	*71% or more*
Journalists	13.0 (3)	43.5 (10)	43.5 (10)

d. How often is the publication of political news constrained by:

	Never	*Rarely*	*Occasionally*	*Frequently*	*Always*
Law	26.1 (6)	56.5 (13)	13.0 (3)		4.3 (1)
Space	4.5 (1)	22.7 (5)	31.8 (7)	18.2 (4)	22.7 (5)
Deadlines	4.3 (1)	17.4 (4)	26.1 (6)	34.8 (8)	17.4 (4)
Source protection	4.3 (1)	21.7 (5)	43.5 (10)	21.7 (5)	8.7 (2)
Other					

e. Of these considerations which, in your experience, constrains the presentation of political news the most?

	Space	Deadlines	Source Protection	Personnel
Journalists	12.5 (3)	20.8 (5)	16.7 (4)	50.0 (12)

f. What would you see as the principal obstacles constraining journalistic investigation in New York? [Mentions]

	Personnel	Time	Access	Complex government	Reader interest	Journalists	Source protection	Party control	Publisher
Journalists	28.1 (9)	18.8 (6)	9.4 (3)	12.5 (4)	6.3 (2)	9.4 (3)	3.1 (1)	3.1 (1)	9.4 (3)

g. Do you think in the public mind that political news from the State level suffers by contrast with the frequency and immediacy of local and/or Washington news?

	Yes	No	Mixed
Journalists	78.3 (18)	4.3 (1)	17.4 (4)

h. If so, can anything be done to change this?

	Quality intrinsic to state news	Editorial perceptions	Personnel problem	Status problem	Journalistic quality
Journalists	13.0 (3)	73.9 (17)		8.7 (2)	4.3 (1)

i. How satisfied are you with the *volume* of State political news that your newspaper normally prints?

	Yes	No	Mixed
Journalists	60.9 (14)	39.1 (9)	

j. Generally speaking, would you say that the press is courted by either legislators or bureaucrats—are favors of any sort offered to you?

	LEGISLATORS		CIVIL SERVANTS		
	Yes	No	Yes	No	Mixed
Journalists	87.0 (20)	13.0 (3)	14.3 (2)	50.0 (7)	35.7 (5)

k. What variations, if any, do you notice in the news situation between Democratic or Republican control of the Legislature and the executive? When Democrats are in control of:

	LEGISLATURE			GOVERNORSHIP		
	None	Some	DK	None	Some	DK
Journalists	27.3 (6)	59.1 (13)	13.6 (3)	18.2 (4)	63.6 (14)	18.2 (4)

l. Can you give examples of the *kind* of lobbyists who seek you out the most—or more frequently? [Mentions]

	Business	Labour	PIGs	Agencies	Legislators	Local governments
Journalists	18.2 (6)	15.2 (5)	54.5 (18)	3.0 (1)	6.0 (2)	3.0 (1)

m. Generally speaking, are there variations in ease of access to news depending on the department or agency concerned? If so, do you have any idea why?

		REASONS	
	Yes	*No*	*Policy area*	*Leadership*
Journalists	87.0 (20)	13.0 (3)	27.3 (6)	72.7 (16)

n. How would you describe your relations with the public information sections of agencies?

	Very good	*Good*	*Satisfactory*	*Unsatisfactory*	*Bad*
Journalists	8.3 (2)	37.5 (9)	29.2 (7)	20.8 (5)	4.1 (1)

o. In general, what is your opinion of the quality of press releases issued by State agencies?

	Very good	*Good*	*Satisfactory*	*Unsatisfactory*	*DK*
Journalists	4.3 (1)	30.4 (7)	30.4 (7)	30.4 (7)	4.3 (1)

p. Do they try to restrict the flow of news by deliberately vague or incomprehensible press releases?

	Yes	*No*	*Sometimes*	*DK*
Journalists	69.6 (16)	8.6 (2)	17.4 (4)	4.3 (1)

q. How often does something you write produce feedback of any sort? If so, which is the biggest source?

	Often	*Sometimes*	*Never*
Journalists	31.8 (7)	68.2 (15)	

| | SOURCES | | | | [MENTIONS] | |
	Public	*Lobbyists*	*Legislators*	*Col-leagues*	*Agencies*	*Editors*
Journalists	15.4 (6)	10.3 (4)	20.5 (8)	15.4 (6)	23.1 (9)	15.4 (6)

r. Do you try to anticipate feedback?

	Frequently	*Sometimes*	*Never*
Journalists	47.8 (11)	17.4 (4)	34.8 (8)

s. Are there restraints on the public's right to know? Do you think certain kinds of stories should be killed?

	Yes	*No*
Journalists	77.3 (17)	22.7 (5)

t. Should public officials be able more easily to claim libel against the media?

	Yes	*No*
Journalists	40.9 (9)	59.1 (13)

Section 3
TRIANGULAR RELATIONSHIPS

8

Legislators, Civil Servants, and Journalists

Journalists are citizens and voters. From time to time all of them have had experience of dealing with legislators or other public officials who may, in their policies or admininstrative acts, very closely mirror their own private views on policy and administration. Equally, they encounter the opposite situation and notice that, despite their professionalism, they can be affronted by views so clearly opposed to their own. Normally, little of either realization finds its way into their news reports, which will be careful attempts at the facts of an issue and the collations of views on it. When journalists have their own columns, of course, they are allowed—expected—to take up clearly stated positions, to defend them, and to expect reactions.

Journalists are *primarily* observers. Their influence, which is undisputed, derives from this role, namely, that of skeptical, informed observers who by publicizing their observations are able on occasion, by constraining or stimulating actors, to alter events in the political arena. In that process newswriters are retailing to the public, and to any special publics, mostly the views of other actors upon whomever or whatever institution is being held up for critical inspection. In so doing, they become communicators between the parts of government and find their outlook on these parts shaped by the criticisms and responses they pass around. If legislators, governors, and civil servants wonder why journalists sometimes seem to have the story written even before an interview, the answer is very simple—journalists know what they are going to say to a large extent because they have said it so often before. In conflicts between parts of government, political parties, or individual leaders, journalists are soaked in the "received wisdom" of the leading actors. They hardly need to ask the parties to a dispute for their views, except to look for signs of change.

New York State provides ample evidence of this in its government, and journalists in Albany are often hard pressed not to be overcome by floods of tired rhetoric. As we saw earlier, the State exhibits classic upstate/downstate, city/suburban tensions and fosters governors who are almost expected to aspire to the presidency. The executive branch is fragmented: its parts have varying degrees of clout with the Legislature, there is a statutory Board of Education that exhibits considerable autonomy. Until 1976 the Legislature had not overridden a gubernatorial veto since 1872 and has tended to have a hard-bitten, patronage-oriented leadership with which a Governor like Rockefeller, with his presidential ambitions and large vision, could harmonize well for most of his years in office. More recently, endorsements of legislators by the Conservative and Liberal parties have given even more colors to the patchwork quilt of cross-cutting localism and, on occasion, even less meaning than usual to the party label. The intricate politics of the Democratic party in New York City and the various strands of rivalry within and between upstate and downstate Republicanism—all meet in the Albany Legislature. When party control differs between the houses in the Legislature and a fiscal crisis looms, then journalists are deluged in rhetoric from the chief executive, a divided legislative leadership, and some agency leaderships—*each* claiming to have differing degrees of popular support and legitimacy. To understand how journalists view such conflicts, we may begin by examining how the legislators and civil servants see each other, and how they see each other's dealings with the media.

Legislators see wide variation in performance between parts of the State bureaucracy; no legislator denied this. On the question of general satisfaction or dissatisfaction with the technical competence of the bureaucracies, legislators were divided, Democrats and Liberals being the most critical.[a] An upstate Democrat spoke of "grave reservations" about many agencies, as did a New York City Democrat, who, however, ended by saying that compared to the "bad city government," the State "gets more work done." Another upstate Democrat charged that the agencies are "not oriented to service, but to the status quo," while an upstate Republican, making the same point, noted that in some agencies "quality equals good press releases." Others from *both* parties talked of the bad precedents set by the Rockefeller administration: "They play divide and rule by keeping the chairman [of a committee] informed and then swearing him to silence." Another legislator, making the same point, added, "Some agencies never see their position as creatures of the Legislature or Governor—if Rocky had confidence in them, then they did not give a hang about anyone."

On the question of the sensitivity of the bureaucracy to the needs of the political leadership—executive and legislative—there seemed greater consensus, one-half of those interviewed claiming that it was not sensitive enough. This question clearly divided Democrats the most—the other three groups, especially Conservatives, being fairly clear on the answer. Being the dominant party currently, and having to rely on the bureaucracy, may have modified traditional Democratic skepticism. When bureaucratic sensitivity to the "needs of the public" was probed, legislators were more certain, some 70 percent claiming to see too much insensitivity. The question evoked particularly unfavorable responses from Democrats, their previous response notwithstanding, while both Liberals and Conservatives—no doubt for opposite reasons—find the posture of the bureaucracy very unsatisfactory in this respect.[b] Both responses give some idea of the distance that legislators see between themselves and civil servants and between civil servants and the public.

Career civil servants, even when senior, see relatively few legislators or their staffs. Most departments or agencies are headed by appointed commissioners, or the equivalent, and any aides they may bring with them. Beyond this level there is the Governor's office and the relevant legislative committee members, especially their chairpersons and ranking members. Taken together, these groups constitute a small number of non-civil servants who impinge directly on their activities—though many legislators may be in touch for information or rule-making purposes. How civil servants see these political leaders and administrators is likely to be important in framing their general attitude toward the political leadership. Considering appointed commissioners and legislators most involved in their policy areas, only 47 percent of civil servants questioned accepted that such people had a competence relevant to the decisions they faced,[c] though 90 percent asserted that they could acquire the competence from within government.[d] However, since nearly as many civil servants believed their competence varied widely, presumably many commissioners and legislators never acquired a relevant competence, as they saw it.[e] It is little wonder, then, that over one-half the civil servants reported that in relation to defining and solving problems in their policy areas, both legislators and commissioners were only of some "assistance." More civil servants, interestingly, were ready to credit legislators—rather than commissioners—with providing "much" assistance.[f]

Clearly, civil servants were highly ambiguous about their legislators' role. Nearly 70 percent of them agreed with the proposition that legislators "play inter-party and intra-party politics with problems most of them barely understand."[g] Those who did not accept this stressed in their answers that only a few legislators—the leadership—counted in decisions and that by the time legislators became leaders they had been socialized into a proper understanding of their role vis-à-vis the bureaucracy: "The more years they are here and the more serious they are, the more they respect us." This must be seen as a posture that raises questions either about the way legislators conduct themselves or about the way civil servants themselves are socialized.

Notwithstanding any personal view journalists might hold, steady exposure to the skepticism, not to say disdain, that clearly exists between legislators and civil servants will tend to make them skeptical of the rhetoric and claims made on behalf of either group.

Exposed to the cross fire of criticism, newswriters try to keep their distance, a task made harder since both groups actively seek to recruit their help and since each is ready to accuse the other of being unhealthily close to a state of manipulating both the press and the public.

Legislators know well the size and proficiency of the public relations offices of most agencies. Indeed, many claim to envy such capacities and to wonder out loud how the Legislature ever allowed them to be built up. The reason is clear: legislators generally believe that public relations has become public management and, worse, legislative management, too. Asked whether the agencies "play the media" for their advantage at the expense of both public and legislators, the answer was almost unanimously yes—only three legislators demurred.[h] The dissenters were Liberals who seemed much more ready to allow the bureaucracy to work for a favorable image via public relations work in the media and elsewhere. On the whole, the agency public relations people were portrayed by legislators as skilled at the news game, particularly in the defense of established policies and wisdom. "Even when they're silent," said one legislator about an agency then under public criticism, "you can be sure that the P.R. boys have advised it since they well know how short the public attention span is."

Civil servants are too well aware that these managerial skills are ascribed by legislators to them. They know that their situation makes them vulnerable to attacks on this, as on other grounds. Asked to characterize legislative attitudes toward them, only 36 percent of the civil servants used terms carrying much warmth or positive feeling ("respect" and "appreciation"), while 45 percent used more negative terms ("hostility," "skepticism," or "exploitation"), and the remainder spoke of a mix of both.[i] Some of the former echoed one who spoke of "trust growing as they see problems solved by the agencies." Others saw suspicion lessening when agencies served "the wishes of legislators in terms of favors for their constituents." The latter group also noted that legislative attitudes were determined by "the political equation" or by the question, "Can they help me?" In this context the commonly held view among civil servants that the media are closer to legislators (physically and sympathetically, because co-opted by them) than to themselves takes on added importance. Sixty percent of the civil servants saw journalists as people whose very activities "contribute to misunderstandings *and* conflict" between them and legislators on occasion.ʲ One wrote that "reporting, by its very nature, incites conflict by focusing on problems and failures." Others took more the line of one who noted that reporters lack understanding and "like to create conflict because it gets a sensational story—a situation which is to their interest." Another observed wearily, "They contribute to misunderstandings about government across *all* lines" (my emphasis). Journalists made worse, on occasion, a situation already fraught with room for conflict and misconceptions and contributed to distorted popular views on the nature of government.

The situation in which journalists find themselves is that they are close to, and are often seen as between, two elites—legislative and bureaucratic—who are skeptical and even at times hostile to each other. Each sees the reporter not so much as a detached, less than neutral observer, but as an independent force that is prone to be too close and sometimes is co-opted by its rival.

The views of the office of the Governor—so far as they may be judged—have elements from both camps. The Governor, too, can find the readiness of mass media to publicize legislative incoherence and personal foibles useful in boosting his own intentions, activities, and standing. He may (privately) rejoice when a recalcitrant entrenched agency is pilloried and may welcome demands that the Governor do something. But, conversely, he may find it necessary to stand behind such an agency when it is being unjustly harried, if only for the sake of general morale. Equally, he may resent media emphasis on the limitations of his power in relation to the agencies or on "his" party in the Legislature. The Governor has his own media interest to develop, and it is to derive maximum support and publicity from both Legislature and bureaucracy while minimizing any damage from either. In his role as legislative leader he (and his staff) may share much of the world view of other legislators. In his role of chief executive, however, the Governor may have to have a much more policy-oriented—and budget-defined—outlook. Not all agencies will share his priorities, and he may resent their ability to say so via the media. Not all journalists or their employers may share his concerns or necessities and are glad to publicize alternatives—from legislators or (more covertly) from within the bureaucracy. The Governor is quite likely to feel that his ideas do not get fair coverage, that journalists "do not understand," or that their employers do not *wish* to understand. Usually they understand only too well; they simply do not share his priorities. Therefore, the Governor and his staff join those who deplore this—until the next issue when the lines may be drawn differently.

Where in all this, then, stand the journalists? First, it is clear that they value their freedom to observe and comment freely very highly indeed. The more they see of the strenuous "management" attempts being directed at them and the more they glimpse the potential juggernaut of united bureaucracies or "whipped," agressive parties, the more they cling to their bedrock right to go behind majorities and official views. Some 41 percent of those interviewed would, in fact, be prepared to see tighter legal control over what they regard as malignant intent in some sorts of press coverage. One upstate reporter thought that freedom of the press did not mean that "journalists should get away with murder." About 60 percent see the present legal situation as perfectly satisfactory, while one or two would have virtually anything said and reported about a public official taken to constitute "fair comment" and to be in the public interest.[k] The attitude in general was summed up by one newsman: "We know the right to privacy is a problem"; but, as another said, "responsible peer group pressure is the way"—not the courts—to deal with the problem.

Journalists do not see the distance between legislators and civil servants as very great. From their perspective the two groups are driven to be very close; there is the need and necessity of their cooperation, the tradition of formal bureaucratic deference to elected officials, and the awareness among legislators of the need to find and keep within agencies the best people they can. Twenty-seven percent of the journalists agree and a further 59 percent strongly agree that legislators and bureaucrats are too cozy with one another—and at the expense of the public.[1] "Sure," said one, "they have to get along," while another talked of politicans "who want rent laws *not* to work because then they can do the favors." For these observers the game of government is played at times with a rhetoric that is at near-total variance with the incremental and accommodative behavior that is the reality in Albany—and is, of course, dictated by the formal system.

For most journalists, it is difficult not to become entangled by the game as defined by its principal players. The side of government that to journalists seems so clearly labeled "for public consumption only" has to be covered—and by them, for they are the first "public" to receive it. They cannot easily ignore bills they know are not intended—far less expected—to pass, nor can they disregard personal news of the political elite or the stage-managed campaign of X or Y agency that feels its image is in need of refurbishing. The activities of the political and bureaucratic elite—whatever it does—are their livelihood, and they are often reminded of it. Yet their profession makes claims to something more, and they know that, too. Journalists are well aware of the dangers of writing for each other or, as bad, of writing with no detachment from their formal assignment as "somebody's reporter in Albany." Without exception, they accepted that they are in a structured triangular relationship with two potent and jealously watchful elites.[m] Each is skeptical of the competence and intentions of the other and jealous of its seemingly undue influence with the press. Each, on occasion (if not often), resents the power of the press and simultaneously covets it for itself. "It is incestuous," one remarked; "they need us and we need them." Another noted how the Albany press corps had a large component of pack journalists so that "reporters can write for reporters not readers." A third commented, "We are too near," and went on to note how the Watergate scandal was unearthed *not* by the *Washington Post's* national political staff, but by two reporters "who were on the Metro team, the police beat."

In turn, the journalists resent the impossibly large size of their task in New York State, the attempts to manage them, and the volume of rhetoric and "pseudo-events" cluttering up their work lives. Except at the level of the local (legislators and their deferential weeklies downstate) or the mundane (rountine noncontentious events), the press-government relationship cannot be characterized by co-optation or its antithesis, a wholly detached, adversary position. Rather, it has components of both; it is dynamic; and, if there is a trend, it seems to be going toward more, rather than less, distance from the elites. If this is the case, then journalists can expect (perhaps to their surprise) that their job will change little. Should the agenda of politics change significantly, they will still have far too much to do if they are conscientious *and* if they are not. The new agenda would still be in jealous hands, and their outsider posture would still earn them hostility and disdain—and demands that they cease favoring the other side. The kitchen would still be hot; and those who did not like it would, one suspects, still long on occasion for the lush, quiet pastures of well-paid legislative or agency public relations work.

Perhaps, however, that is an overly journalistic perspective. Perhaps those lush pastures are not so lush when entered upon. Perhaps there are yet other perspectives on the legislative-civil service-journalistic relationship that may usefully be examined? What, for example, do the various aides think of the performance of these groups, and what are the views of editors in radio/television stations and newspapers?

DATA

Figures in parentheses = n
All others = %
Party affiliation   Legislators only

a. Generally speaking are you satisfied with the technical competence of the State bureaucracies? If not, why?

	Very satisfied	Satisfied	Dissatisfied	Very Dissatisfied	Mixed
Legislators	3.4 (1)	48.3 (14)	38.0 (11)		10.3 (3)
Democrats		40.0 (6)	53.3 (8)		6.7 (1)
Republicans	7.1 (1)	57.1 (8)	21.4 (3)		14.3 (2)
Liberals		25.0 (2)	62.5 (5)		12.5 (1)
Conservatives		44.4 (4)	33.3 (3)		22.2 (2)

b. Do you think that the bureaucracy, in the context of its press relations, is sensitive enough to (1) the needs of the public; (2) the needs of the political leadership, both legislative and executive?

	PUBLIC				POLITICAL LEADERSHIP			
	Yes	No	Mixed	DK	Yes	No	Mixed	DK
Legislators	10.3 (3)	72.4 (21)	13.8 (4)	3.4 (1)	27.6 (8)	55.2 (16)	13.8 (4)	3.4 (1)
Democrats	7.1 (1)	85.7 (12)	7.1 (1)		40.0 (6)	46.7 (7)	6.7 (1)	6.7 (1)
Republicans	13.3 (2)	60.0 (9)	20.0 (3)	6.7 (1)	14.3 (2)	64.3 (9)	21.4 (3)	
Liberals	12.5 (1)	75.0 (6)	12.5 (1)		25.0 (2)	62.5 (5)	12.5 (1)	
Conservatives		77.8 (7)	22.2 (2)			77.8 (7)	22.2 (2)	

c. In general, do both groups have a competence that is *relevant* to the decisions they face?

	Yes	No	Very mixed
C. Servants	47.0 (8)	29.4 (5)	23.5 (4)

d. If not, do they have the resources to acquire that competence?

	Usually	Sometimes	Rarely	Never
C. Servants	92.3 (12)	7.7 (1)		

e. Does their capacity and assistance vary by area of government activity?

	Very much	Usually
C. Servants	81.2 (13)	18.8 (3)

f. In your decision making, in the defining of problems, and in the educating of the public to accept necessary solutions, how much assistance do your expect from (1) legislators; (2) non-civil-service commissioners, etc.?

	LEGISLATORS			COMMISSIONERS		
	Much	Some	None	Much	Some	None
C. Servants	37.5 (6)	56.2 (9)	6.3 (1)	23.1 (3)	61.5 (8)	15.4 (2)

g. Generally speaking, would you agree that legislators "play inter-party and intra-party politics with problems most of them barely understand"?

	Strongly agree	Agree	Disagree	Strongly disagree	Mixed
C. Servants	27.8 (5)	38.9 (7)	16.7 (3)	16.7 (3)	16.7 (3)

h. Do you think the bureaucracy "plays" the media for its advantage at the expense of (1) legislators; (2) the public?

	LEGISLATORS			PUBLIC		
	Yes	No	Mixed	Yes	No	Mixed
Legislators	88.9 (24)		11.1 (3)	88.9 (24)		11.1 (3)
Democrats	85.7 (12)		14.3 (2)	85.7 (12)		14.3 (2)
Republicans	92.3 (12)		7.7 (1)	92.3 (12)		7.7 (1)
Liberals	75.0 (6)		25.0 (2)	75.0 (6)		25.0 (2)
Conservatives	88.9 (8)		11.1 (1)	88.9 (8)		11.1 (1)

i. In your experience what characterizes the attitudes of legislators toward bureaucrats?

	Respect	Hostility	Skepticism	Appreciation	Exploitation	Mixed
C. Servants	18.2 (4)	22.7 (5)	13.6 (3)	18.2 (4)	9.1 (2)	18.2 (4)

j. How often, would you say, do journalists by their activities contribute to misunderstandings *and* conflict between bureaucrats and legislators?

	Occasionally	Never	Mixed
C. Servants	57.9 (11)	10.5 (2)	31.6 (6)

k. Should public officials be able more easily to claim libel against the media?

	Yes	No
Journalists	40.9 (9)	59.0 (13)

l. How far is it possible to see legislators and bureaucrats as too "cozy" with one another at the expense of the public?

	Strongly agree	Agree	Disagree	Strongly disagree
Journalists	59.1 (13)	27.3 (6)	4.5 (1)	9.0 (2)

m. How far is it possible to see yourselves and the legislators and bureaucracies as engaged in a triangular relationship with the general public in the role of distant and ill-informed onlooker?

	Strongly agree	Agree	Disagree	Strongly disagree
Journalists	63.6 (14)	36.4 (8)		

9

Editors, Aides, and Reporters

Reporters may be engaged in what we have termed a triangular relationship with legislators and civil servants. They are also simultaneously engaged in a similar relationship with two other sets of people who are very important in their lives. These are the editors at newspapers or radio and television stations who use their news and the press aides around the Governor, legislators, and agency heads. Reporters are, in many senses, poised between the aides, who—often despite themselves—supply a great deal of their news, and the editors, who cut what reporters produce to fit their own editorial needs. We need to look more closely at both groups, at their attitudes toward government and politics in New York State, and at media roles and performance within that setting.

The importance of the news editor seems clear. New York State political news, so far as the mass media are concerned, is what is printed, spoken, or shown and *not* what might have been printed, spoken, or shown. The decision to use or not use copy from the wire services or from reporters is a critical judgement that is routinized by the editorial staff. What those around the Governor, in the agencies, and in the Legislature think of the media will relate to the attention given to news they themselves release to the media or to what they cannot stop being said about their activities in the media. As a gate keeper in the process of converting information into news, the editor is a crucial link since it is his or her job to assemble the news on a day-by-day basis. Despite understandings with the newspaper's reporter at Albany, if there is one, no news is sacred to an editor. The "play" that news is given—where it is put, how it is placed on a page, whether it receives editorial treatment—all are decisions that the Albany reporter has a share in and no more. Yet, such decisions are vital to the impact of news. We have seen that many of the key actors in State politics regard the editor as a much more significant factor in determining what actually appears in the media than the reporter who covers the State in Albany, or elsewhere.

The importance of the various media aides, as seen by the political and bureaucratic elite, is testified to by the numbers that are employed and also by the fact that at the highest levels the media aide has become a general purpose aide.[1] Indeed, most of those interviewed for this study claimed that an increasing share of their work was of a general advisory capacity. They have already become advisers on the effect of policy and, hence, increasingly advisers on *which* policies should be adopted to achieve desired effects. That public relations can degenerate into an activity fostering "backing into" policy in this way is a danger the aides were aware of.[2] In any event, such individuals are ardent consumers of political news in any form. As ex-journalists, often in more than one medium, their perspectives are important for several reasons. First, of course, they know the news game and can assess the way journalists play it with a professional eye. Second, their assessments are usually conveyed directly to the principal actors in any government situation and can have a significant molding effect on the views of those actors. Last, but not least, the frequent interaction of these aides with their former colleagues—for leaks, corrections, or whatever—can be more influential in molding the views of newswriters than many of them admit even to themselves. The aides, in short, are a valuable, and sometimes vital, link in the chain of influence between the officials, the mass media, and the mass public.

Both groups, then, are well placed for being influential. Who are they? In their general characteristics the editors seemed little different from the press corps at the capitol and confirmed the impression that journalism is a youthful profession.[3] Almost all were under forty-five years of age, and over half were under thirty-five. In terms of background, just over one-third were from out of State, and a similar proportion had graduated from journalism school. Virtually all had a B.A. degree with a history, English, or political science major. Very few had previous Albany experience.

The aides showed some noticeable contrasts.[4] Their average age was higher, nearer forty-five years of age, in fact. Three-quarters of them had been in the print press, over half of those in the capitol press corps and more than half of those with work experience for the wire services. In addition to a print press background, three of them had also worked in radio and television. All except one had completed their college education, usually with a political science or English major. Four had further qualifications, three having M.A.'s and one having earned an LL.B. All three groups—reporters, editors, and aides—showed closely matching characteristics. The most significant difference was, of course, that the average age rises as one moves from reporters, through editors, to aides.

What do these groups read? The news editors reported reading a spread of national newspapers and magazines (*Wall Street Journal, Christian Science Monitor, Time, Newsweek*) and some other regional papers within the State. On a daily basis, however, the Associated Press, United Press International, and the *New York Times* appeared to be mandatory reading for news editors. An upstate editor noted that the important papers for him were "the *Times,* Albany, Buffalo, because the government officials are keyed to these." True or not for him, news editors generally did not report reading Albany and Buffalo newspapers, they presumably relied on the *Times* and the wire to pick up any of their stories. The aides reported a similar reliance on the *New York Times* and the wire services. If they were legislative aides, they also reported reading a large number of local papers in their particular legislator's district. Again, they had access to extensive statewide clipping services kept by the legislative leaderships. News editors have a great deal of other political, as well as nonpolitical, news to consider besides New York State political news. Aides have a narrower focus, namely, their own legislator, district, or agency, and may ignore nonpolitical news. They monitor radio and television coverage for spot news and, as will be seen, for any special coverage that is devoted to their particular area of interest.

Before we can consider the attitudes of both editors and aides toward the performance of the mass media, we need to examine their attitudes toward State government and politics in general. We cannot avoid beginning with their attitudes toward the Rockefeller era.

News editors, perhaps because of their distance from Albany both during and since the Rockefeller years, are the most tentative on his impact. Whereas over 80 percent of the legislators and aides and nearly that number of reporters believe that Rockefeller dazzled the media with his news management and virtually co-opted reporters, only one-half of the editors believe this. Most of the aides, of course, were reporters when Rockefeller was Governor and are, self-confessedly, marked by that period. They believe that they were part of the process of creating the image of the Rockefeller era and that, in effect, the Governor was able to manage their access to news. More than one-half of them see the Rockefeller legacy in media-government relations as one of tight control and manipulation of journalists. As one agency aide commented, "He commanded the news; he always made the news personally or by what his releases said . . . He used "blitzes." . . . it was considered that you usually had to run these stories just because they came from the Governor." Importantly, the aides saw that the legacy was short-lived. In their view, the access to news had sharply increased and the capacity to manage the media by politicians had sharply decreased. The aides' assessments of current media performance must be seen in this light, namely, that the Rockefeller era has ended and reporters have a great opportunity to regain their independence. A legislative aide concluded a diatribe on the current level of access for the press by stating that in contrast "Rockefeller had no particular probing—he was not the recipient of today's distrust." Be that as it may, it is interesting to note that despite their conviction that the situation has changed in New York State, aides seemed still to expect the strong gubernatorial style to be dominant and were only half as sure as legislators (43 percent against 80 percent) that a strongly led Legislature can substitute for it.

In this context, then, what may we say of State political news and the role of the media? Is State news overshadowed in the public mind by local and Washington news, they were asked. Legislators and reporters thought so, as was seen. Even more so was this the conviction of the aides. In some contrast, the editors disagreed, 60 percent of them asserting that State news was not so overshadowed. This, interestingly, is the position of the only respondents in this study who are located outside Albany. Aides, reporters certainly, and even legislators may socialize one another into a common perception of the way in which State news is unfairly treated. We saw in chapter 2 that State news (in terms of volume) in the press is, except in the Albany newspapers, usually a smaller proportion of political news than local, national, and international news. It may be that editors are reflecting on the likely increase in State news in the future, whereas the others are reflecting on past coverage and their belief that things will continue as they are.

How large a role do the media play in securing nominations and winning elections? Here again, there is some contrast. Whereas aides (and legislators and reporters) were ready to concede a large role for the media in winning elections, they saw a smaller role in winning nominations. Not so the editors, who claimed a larger role in the nominating process and a large role in the election process. The contrast, of course, could result from editorial blindness or from a lively sense of their own importance. It could be, too, another example of the distance from Albany exhibited by these editors, who have very little share in the hothouse atmosphere of the State Capitol. Editorial staffs in the statewide media have a higher view of their own political importance than do the Albany press corps or even the members of the Legislature.

Certainly in their attitudes toward the State Legislature and agencies the editors evince considerable superiority. News editors appear not to be overly enthusiastic on the branches of the State government. They are more than twice as ready as reporters in Albany to assert that the State is less than well served by political parties and politicians (60 percent, compared to 26 percent). Among aides the pattern of responses approximates much more closely that of reporters. Thus, the aides were as skeptical as journalists of the services rendered to the State by legislators (53 percent versus 56 percent). One aide, for example, noted that the Legislature ''is managed by a few older leaders; new members are denied much participation. . . . minor items are too prevalent."

More than one-quarter of the editors felt that the State was not well served by the agencies, and a further 50 percent characterized the State as being only "fairly well served" by them. This was, of course, a generalization covering a wide variety of performance. As one senior editor put it, "Some [agencies] . . . are excellent, others . . . are frightful." Among the aides, too, there was as great a skepticism of the quality of the State civil service. One legislative aide noted that excess bureaucracy "breeds on itself and needs stifling," while another observed wearily, "The media . . . could help open up the agencies . . . but don't." From inside the agency the view of one aide was much more explicit. There was "overspending: much of it due to poor control over funds. Government is a huge source of funds for private contractors and other interests."

It is against this background, then, that we may set the more technical assessments of the situation and performance of the media. The news situation following the departure of Rockefeller, the pressing fiscal crisis, the mixed performance of both Legislature and agencies as seen by each other—taken together, these should present great opportunity to the media. How have they taken advantage of it, at least as seen by editors and aides?

To begin, let us look at the question of access. As we saw earlier, legislators believe there is "too much" access, while journalists themselves accept that the State is adequately accessible. Aides overwhelmingly agree (90 percent) that access is adequate. Sixty percent of editors, however, disagreed and stressed how much further the State has to go in the area of accessibility. Once again we may be looking here at the non-Albany viewpoint, or at one that does not reflect recent changes in access, or at one that does not reflect the *actual* situation prevailing in Albany.

The aides, anyway, were more concerned to emphasize (nearly 50 percent of them) the limited capacity of the press corps to exploit the access they have and to preserve the access they have by respecting confidentiality. One legislative aide noted wryly that the ability of reporters to exploit access was not as great as their ability "to talk about it." Nine-tenths of the aides claimed good personal relations with the press. A very senior legislative aide put his relations down principally to the fact that "my years of experience help me anticipate their questions." More than four-fifths of the aides supported a position of "open government" so far as journalists are concerned. Yet more than one-third of them were concerned over the reliability and trustworthiness of journalists in their treatment of news sources. One agency aide noted that "decency they accept grudgingly," while a legislative aide claimed to see the rapid decline of humor and trust. "There are," he said, "too many reporters you cannot talk to—you can't kid with those guys any more." Interview experience suggests that some aides held such views before leaving journalism, while others clearly had changed their views in their new jobs.

Perhaps some echoes of these attitudes are seen in the responses of editors to the constraints they see in covering State political news. Space considerations are important, but much more so are the limits imposed by personnel. These are defined by them more in terms of quality, than quantity. One editor spoke of the need for "competent and responsible reporting capable of researching and interpreting complex issues and circumstances." Another editor was more direct, stating that "too many journalists [print and broadcast] are under-paid "hacks" who achieve their position by longevity and inability to progress." Overall, however, editors still feel they retain considerable freedom of choice over State news. The most potent constraint is their notion of the newsworthiness of State news, which relates to what *they* perceive the public wishes to read, see, or hear about. In their eyes State news is *clearly* more newsworthy recently, but for substantive, not reportorial, reasons. Thus, 70 percent of them are satisfied or very satisfied with the volume of State news they now put out. Here, at least, they had the support of the legislators, 60 percent of whom had no quarrel with the volume of State news printed.

By contrast, 40 percent of the reporters were not satisfied with the volume of news, and neither were most of the aides (62 percent). Even more than the legislators, the aides stressed the large areas of government that are simply ignored by reporters and expressed general dissatisfaction with the volume of coverage of State government and politics in the mass media. A senior legislative aide observed that by taking the "hard" news, television and radio had forced newspapers to concentrate on "background analysis." He went on to add that, in any case, "some editors don't want the

State 'nitty gritty' news, but the news they haven't heard themselves." Another noted how reporters follow their own interests and ignore the larger public. As an example, he cited "young newsmen ignoring old people to the extent that we have senior citizens who are not aware of what the State offers."

What about the relationship between the mass media—in particular, that between the press and television? On this issue there is some contrast in the responses. The aides, overwhelmingly drawn from the print press, stress that it continues to be the most significant medium for State politics—though they seem less sure of this than the press corps itself (50 percent versus 65 percent). An agency aide remarked that although press coverage is being upstaged by television, legislators "still give it weight . . . because it is a record," while another aide asserted that since television coverage was ignoring government, "the print press is as vital as ever." They recognize the critical importance of the *New York Times*, but, more than journalists, stress also the political clout of the other dailies in the State. One legislative aide pointed out that there was a hierarchy "in media minds—but not in people's minds." For him a news entry in the *New York Times* meant "prestige . . . not impact."

Nearly 90 percent of the editors believe television to be the most significant medium, and in this they sharply contrast with Albany reporters. Yet, interestingly, they agree that the processes of government are not very telegenic and hence, arguably, are better covered by the press. They report no feedback on the impact of the single most concentrated television program concerned with State news, namely, the Public Broadcasting System's (PBS) "Inside Albany." This response may be a reflection of the dominance of editors in commercial television stations among respondents and, also, of the novelty of the PBS program. Interview experience in Albany strongly suggests that the program has been defined as important by legislators since its inception. Thus, there is a puzzling element—and there remains the feeling that these respondents are relatively unaware of developments at Albany. One television editor noted that government was "as telegenic as the people making the news." Most Albany reporters would reply that political news is not so easily televised and would ask, How do you televise a decision *not* reached or one that is fudged? The danger is clear:

State news on television can become, as one editor put it, "to those uninterested . . . a monumental bore . . . a parade of talking heads."

Earlier it was noted that more than half the legislators were concerned to stress the limitations on the editorial functions of media, particularly the press. When aides were asked to define the proper role of the media in the State government and politics, they stressed, as did civil servants, the editorial/educational role *even more* than did journalists themselves. One legislative aide was emphatic that the media should "accept their role in explaining government to the people," while another stressed that the media "must be a watchdog—but an educator too." Editors, of course, have no doubt at all about their right to editorialize, though four-fifths of them stressed the necessity of maintaining the traditional distinction between fact and comment.

Editors were equally clear that in exercising their editorial roles, they were not contributing to the entrenchment of localistic attitudes that made statewide mobilization of opinion difficult to achieve. Whereas over four-fifths of Albany reporters saw the media as reinforcing parochialism, nearly 60 percent of the editors disagreed or strongly disagreed with the proposition. One editor commented, "we need less group ownership and cross-ownership, but it is an economic fact we will continue to live with."

By contrast, four-fifths of the aides accepted the fact of a media contribution to localism. One aide noted that the "local angle clouds the coverage." Another aide added, however, that "government tends to self-insulation; the press is a good corrective." Here, very clearly, is reflected the gap in perception between those whose focus is statewide at Albany and those whose jobs have socialized them into a locally oriented frame of reference. Seen from any one locality, the State must tend to be the sum of its parts. To those whose vantage point is Albany, that may be true; but it becomes an insufficient basis on which to frame public policy.

The triangular relationship of the aides, reporters, and editors is, inevitably, tensest in the area of news gathering. Here, formally at least, editors and reporters are ranged on one side, with aides on the other. Editors were in little doubt about the relationship of reporters and government in the post-Watergate atmosphere. They doubted whether reporters were much affected by Watergate, whereas 80 percent of the reporters claimed to be "much" affected by those events. One skeptic noted that Watergate had affected the professionals "not at all," but, he added "journalism schools are overflowing." If one believes this, it is hardly surprising that editors, when asked whether public officials needed more legal protection against the media, should be more ready than reporters to assert that they did not (76 percent versus 60 percent). Given editors' views on the quality of reporters, it is not surprising that they should view any further legal protection as further excuse for journalistic incapacity or inactivity.

Seen from the other side of the field of conflict, the view was, perhaps inevitably, somewhat different. More than legislators (72 percent), aides felt that Watergate had had considerable effect on reporters, not at all for the better. For them the rise of investigative journalism had led too often to much deliberate confusion of fact and inference. A senior legislative aide remarked that since Watergate, "criticism has become ham-fisted, not subtle"; and another added primly that reporters "have other duties besides so-called exposés." Since so often the aides have to deal directly with the press on a confidential basis, it may not be surprising that three-fourths of them claim to have been hurt by unfair practice by reporters. One senior agency aide, who denied having been hurt himself by the press, added that to avoid trouble "we've learned not to be too cozy with the press." Another noted that Watergate was "heady—a realization of power" for newswriters, while a colleague added tartly that "Katie Graham was unhappy about reporters looking at the *Washington Post itself.*" This obviously is a reflection of the difficulties they meet in being close, but guarded, with former colleagues. The reporters have in fact become for aides what they have long been for many legislatsors—namely, the friendly, or not so friendly, adversaries of those in government. As we saw earlier, the element of *personal* trust between reporters and aides has been endangered, a fact of more long-term consequence to reporters than aides, as the former admit. Few aides claim to regard the media as frequently manipulated by those in government; only 15 percent regard this as a frequent or routine occurrence. They appear more psychologically detached than either the politicians or the journalists, who are united in their desire to make the front page, albeit mostly for opposed reasons. One legislative aide noted that though legislators "do everything legal to get news," the incidence of strategic manipulation of the press was rare, only "three or four times a year—and you could defend it."

Yet if aides believe that the media are not manipulated by those in government as easily as journalists may fear, those same aides are not slow to point out that manipulation of other kinds does take place. Whereas legislators were quick to highlight press inaccuracies (52 percent had some doubts), and to claim personal experience of misrepresentation (78 per cent), aides were much less inclined to do so (14 percent and 64 percent, respectively).

It was not that these aides regarded the coverage of State news as "fairer" than did legislators. Instead, the aides were concerned to stress selective or inadvertent omission of fact, rather than inaccurate or distorted presentation of news, as the cause of unfairness. Generally, they were nearly twice as likely as legislators to cite this mode as the way bias is introduced into news stories (60 percent versus 21 percent). Speaking of a recent "scandal" involving clients of the agency, one senior agency aide commented that "we held briefings for newsmen on a regular basis." He went on to note that, nevertheless, even among reporters he respected, " conjecture was made into fact, and sins of omission into those of commission." A legislative aide stated that while the Albany press corps showed "higher accuracy than in Washington, D.C.," he personally always distinguished between that of the "accurate upstate press" and the "inaccurate New York City press." The reason for the distinction, he said, was that "New York City is shock-proof, the reporters know it, and hence they write with that in mind."

Why does bias of this sort occur? Generally, three-fifths of the aides could agree with a similar proportion of legislators—even with reporters, for that matter—that it seems to be an integral part of the news-gathering process. Within this framework, however, half the legislators and aides are prepared to give reporters a share of the blame. The aides are much less likely to add in interviews that, of course, the publishers or editors are "really to blame." As ex-reporters themselves, they seem much less ready to see responsibility placed anywhere but on the shoulders of reporters.

The responses of the aides to questions on the origins of bias in news reporting are interesting in that they can expose their underlying attitudes toward newswriters and the news-gathering function itself. Generally speaking, it is true to say that the agency aides were less critical of the media and less analytical. The scant coverage that most agencies secure has much to do with this. Most agency aides agreed with reporters that government, though increasingly important, is less newsworthy than rhetorical conflict in the Legislature and is much harder to cover. For the agency aide, the primary struggle is to secure *any* coverage, not one to ensure wholly accurate coverage. Legislative aides were mostly at the opposite pole. Privately they would probably prefer less, but more accurate, coverage of their employees and their activities. Their responses revealed a range of reactions to media coverage.

First, a minority claim to see political partisanship. This charge was relatively rare, and the assertions were usually directed at reporters rather than media institutions. One senior legislative aide said, without too much rancor, that "most journalists are Democrats"; variations on this theme were expressed by others. Publishers, however, did not escape entirely. Another legislative aide described the *New York Times* as partisan because of "its socially conscious family ownership." Repetition of the *New York Times's* masthead quotation with acid, often scathing emendations was frequent in interviews.

Second, most aides talked of more complex partisanship arising from the structure of media ownership. For these aides the problem of coverage is, as one said, that "the ownership will not allow a costly, adequate job" or, as another observed, that ownerships "sell papers *and* injustices along the way." Given the commercially oriented ownerships of newspapers and radio/television stations, he felt it was clear that there existed a situation in which "you don't sell papers by telling people how good everybody is—there has to be a crisis." Reporters are, thus, the agents of owners whose interest in political news is a product of their commercial needs. One senior aide noted that the process of acculturation of reporters begins early: "On the weeklies the young journalist learns to write as he thinks the boss wants, and most journalists begin on weeklies, since dailies won't take greenhorns." He agreed with another legislative aide, who commented that government is an easy target for such ownerships, because "you won't get sued, and you can attack with impunity."

A third type of response—the most widespread—was the criticism by aides of reporters and their situation. From their own experience and observation, *all* the aides claimed to see evidences of pack journalism and ego-centeredness among journalists. One aide stated that newswriters "develop a cult and feed off each other," while a second added that "they outdo each other in trivial vision." Other aides talked of the "up for the session" mentality they claimed to be so visible within the press corps and echoed criticisms made even by reporters themselves that some stories were written "before the event." As one aide noted, "they ask *us* for evidence for *their* theories." Journalistic prima donnas easily arouse their ire. One very senior aide singled out a leading member of the press corps who "thinks he has been ordained to be *the* critic" of the Legislature and added that too many reporters saw themselves in that role. It was, he said, for them a job that had become "like covering the opera, or the bullfights." Again, a minority of aides were quick to criticize editorial writers. As one put it, they "gain knowledge from what they read in their own newspapers" and then expect their reporters to find evidence to support "the position *they* have taken up."

What are the consequences of this mix of characteristics, at least as seen by aides? Most of them are clear that from time to time the media hinder political communication in New York State and contribute to misunderstandings between legislators, the Governor, and the agencies. One legislative aide noted, "We're portrayed as bickering politicians, and bureaucrats sometimes look down on us." More generally, as another aide claimed, the media portray an image of the Legislature that is not conducive to recruiting good staff: "Reporters do not help us get staff, and we need them."

The recital of journalistic omissions is, of course, at least as illuminating on the aides as it is on the reporters. A lack of understanding of the task of the reporter—when faced with incomplete and often suspect information, with limited resources to check that information, and with pressing deadlines—is clear. Reporters' attempts to collate various sources and to check the veracity of some of them constitute what the aide quoted earlier called "theories" for which he resented being asked to supply "evidence." Squeezed by aides who are reluctant to exert themselves to supply information and editors who demand "a day's copy for a day's pay," reporters not surprisingly, are, often scathing on both and despair of doing anything but the rushed job that is so apt to result in errors and injustices.

How do editors view the triangular relationship between legislators, agencies, and reporters? How is the Albany news game seen from afar by editors? Certainly they appear to be in no doubt on the legislative-agency relationship, which they see as too close, too cozy, for the good of the public. Where reporters fitted into this is not, it seems, so clear. The editors are equally divided on the question of whether reporters are too close to the Legislature and the agencies for their own good and that of the public. As before, distance lends uncertainty to the view. In truth, many editors do not know the quality of the relationship, do not know, in fact, what it is like to be a reporter in Albany. One editor, at least, was quite clear that the relationship of media and government is too close. Seen from his perspective, however, closeness "can't be avoided . . .[for] the media is a bureaucracy too."

Whatever the situation is, it is unlikely to change in the future. We saw earlier that few newswriters (22 percent) expect much change in the political geography of New York State. By comparison, some 40 percent of the aides expected to see more two-party competition and, as interview experience suggests, much more conflict in general. Editors are even more convinced, it appears, that change is likely, nine-tenths of them claiming to see new issues and more two-party competition ahead for the State. One upstate editor put his view of future political developments tersely: "Isolation for New York City." Another argued that "party labels would become more meaningless as more eyes will turn to Washington."

Asked what role the media will play in any significant political change, fully two-thirds of the editors seemed to think the role could be an important one and would occur in the near future. In the words of one editor, "It will force the media more and more to represent the public," while another claimed that the press "will more closely monitor public spending." His paper, he claimed, was "now considerably more aggressive in our dealings with officials. . . . As a consequence we find ourselves criticized for ignoring the 'news.' "

Aides and editors exhibit an interesting mix of journalistic and nonjournalistic perspectives. Both groups are, in some senses, *former* reporters, since they are no longer actually in the field. One group had gone on to manage reporters, the other to join government. The latter had come to see newswriters as would a legislator or a civil servant. The responses of editors are redolent with received wisdom. Editors are distant from the day-by-day attrition, conflict, and often bored weariness of reporters and they sound like it. The aides, in their closeness, are the reverse. Occasionally, they give the impression of seeing *only* newswriters scrambling for a story at any price. Editors tend to see their reporters in Albany as abstractions at work, while aides see only working reporters and forget the abstract principles that can motivate them.

NOTES

1. The Department of Civil Service reported 90 public information specialists between grades 14 and 25 in August 1976. (Figures taken from the *New York State Government Public Relations Association Directory, 1975* and updated to August 1976 by the Department.) In addition, the department lists separately ten public relations officers and assistant commissioners for public relations. Those need to be distinguished from other senior aides who perform both public relations and general purpose advisory functions, but who sit under other titles. It is interesting that both aides and reporters agree that such people are found in almost all agencies. The total number of public relations functionaries could then be as high as 120, of whom some 50—however described—would have sufficient status to be independently influential. In the Legislature and the Governor's entourage, similarly, there is an overlap between public relations and general purpose aides. With this in mind, estimates among journalists run to 30 individuals at leadership levels and between 50 and 60 covering the Legislature generally.

2. See chap. 3, above, pp. 34-36 for a discussion of this.

3. Questionnaires were mailed to news editors of all New York State-based television stations and to all newspapers with a circulation of over 40,000. Of the fifty-nine mailed out, nineteen were returned, making a 32 percent sample. For both editors and aides the questions asked were the same as in chaps. 4-10, inclusive.

4. Fifteen aides were interviewed. All were identified by LCA members as key influentials, or they identified each other. They ranged from individuals in the Governor's office through those in Senate and Assembly, and, finally, some were drawn from large and/or controversial agencies. This is not a proper sample, but a leadership-oriented group showing a remarkable homogeneity of attitude.

10
Conclusions

After one press conference for which Press Secretary Ron Maiorana had briefed the governor on 50 questions, Rockefeller tweaked the reporters with the observation: "You only asked 15 questions—Ron had 35 more." With needles like that, one veteran legislative correspondent said, "he was the best person at fondling and diverting the press."[1]

Governments, ultimately, have to mobilize support (or manage dissent), and the mass media, imperfect as they seem, are among the first targets for their mobilization efforts. This examination of the attitudes of many of the key actors in the process of political communication in New York State has revealed something of a triangle of distrust, if not disdain. It may well be that such attitudes are only to be expected in media-government relations, particularly in a political system that prescribes separated institutions of government, but shared powers. Since only too recently there has been clear evidence of aggrandizing tendencies in the executive branch at the national level, and since the media publicized—if not first discovered—such evidence, this has only intensified latent tensions between journalists and elected and appointed officials. If the American system needed evidence of the importance of a free press, then Watergate provided it.

In New York State the timing of the Watergate episode was possibly of more local importance than in many states, since it coincided with the departure of Governor Nelson Rockefeller and a progressive reassessment of his achievements. As we have seen, assessments and reassessments of Rockefeller's style and achievements lie, often unstated, behind many of the responses reported in this study. Any Governor who held office as long as Rockefeller did would have had considerable influence on media-government relations. In Rockefeller's case there is the added dimension that he was an exceptionally strong-minded manager of the executive and the legislative branches. President Nixon would have envied such a tightly run executive and well-managed Legislature.

The aftermath of the Watergate scandals and the Rockefeller era made it likely that media-government relations in the State would exhibit much uncertainty as the newly released hopes and fears of journalists and officials coincided or conflicted. We have seen how both legislators and civil servants ascribe great importance to the mass media, but claim to see considerable inaccuracy and bias in the way political news is reported in the State. Both groups—but legislators especially—are ready to blame publishers and reporters for this bias and claim that post-Watergate so-called investigative journalism has increased the incidence of biased reporting. Four-fifths of both groups claim *personal* experience of being misreported in ways that lead them to ascribe causes other than error to the newswriters and their newspapers or stations. Both groups see the media as having been either vulnerable to or willing to lend themselves to Rockefeller's manipulation and image building. Legislators and civil servants do not fail to note that the media were, for example, not as ardent for the recent Freedom of Information Act as were various good government groups. This accords with their experience that reporters are only too ready *not* to attend committee meetings, press conferences, and the like and makes them even more skeptical of the overblown rhetoric that the media indulge in either about their rights or their day-to-day performance.

The other side of this coin is not less clear. Reporters, but not editors, are more cautious in claiming such large influence for themselves or their newspapers or stations. As for bias, reporters are quick to note that legislators and civil servants are often ready to practice "selective memory" about what they themselves have said, especially if the words they used have had unintended effects for them. As for increased access, reporters argue that this simply increases their obligations to their editors and the public (more meetings to attend, more documents to see) while doing nothing to increase their resources of staff and time. Further, they argue that legislators and civil servants, who are quick to criticize pack journalism, should realize that the pack is a way of responding to the pack-like realities reporters must face when they meet legislative parties, factions, agency cliques, and so on. Repeatedly, as we saw, newswriters stress the capabilities of both legislators and agencies to mislead them and the public via their public relations staffs.

At the end of the day, however, the groups of journalists, legislators, and civil servants are not monolithic. Each is composed of individuals who optimize their relationships with members of other groups as best they can. Thus, for legislators there are trustworthy reporters and a larger number who are either not worthy of trust or simply not known. Likewise, civil servants pick and choose their reporters; and the latter, in turn, distinguish sharply between reliable and unreliable sources. Notwithstanding *general* distrust, then, there are networks of *particular* trust and reliance. Moreover, of course, there are those in each group who urge change on members of other groups, safe in the knowledge (or hope) that such change will not happen or will happen only in ways they approve of. Thus, some legislators can advocate tough media scrutiny of the agencies, but would be unhappy if such scrutiny were directed at them. Likewise, in the comments of both civil servants and journalists, there are elements of posturing and the unexpressed satisfaction that things are not worse or less tolerable. As always, in an ongoing system the elements of plain *comfort* with things as they are must not be overlooked. Certainly the latter are visible in Albany, whatever any of the participants may claim. Indeed, these characteristics have recently been criticized in terms that stressed precisely the qualities of coziness, of the happy adjustment of the groups to each other.[2]

The overall picture of media-government relations in the State is, as might be expected, a multifaceted reality and one that bears out the general framework established by earlier work, in particular that of Delmer Dunn.[3] Like Dunn, this study found that elective and appointive officials seek to recruit members of the press into active, participatory roles when that suits them. Conversely, it was seen that both are quick to complain that Albany reporters are ready to be participants *only,* and are unwilling to be neutral transmitters of information to the public. As did Dunn, this study discovered that perspectives on the media vary by the needs of the observers. Thus, legislators regard the media as a useful counterweight to agency inertia, incompetence, or corruption, while civil servants regard media as a valuable check on excessive influence wielded by special or parochial interests in the Legislature. Again, it was noted how legislators share with newswriters a conflict outlook and were more tolerant of journalistic insistence that there were always two sides to every question. Conversely, civil servants were more anxious to keep actual or potential conflicts within agencies until they were ready to go public with agreed solutions. Evidence also revealed that such a style aroused the resentment of legislators and journalists, both groups regarding such behavior as always presenting them with faits accomplis.

The consequences for the mass media of the largeness and complexity of New York State government are amply borne out. As in Washington, so in Albany there can be great gulfs of perception between elective and appointive officials and their staffs. They cannot, as in Wisconsin, be gathered in one large hall, far less in one room. The media are looked to as a supplement of intragovernmental communications systems and are used as an arena for offensive and defensive "plays" by officials who, unlike their counterparts in Wisconsin, do not feel that they are in control of the whole situation. Thus, as noted in chapter 1, the media have secondary communication roles: stories ostensibly aimed at the public are in reality aimed at other officials whose attention and response was the prime reason for the release of the story in the first place. The more stress that exists in these large complex organizations, the more likely are the media to be used in this way, whether they know it or not.

The roles of the mass media in the policymaking process are varied and have not been well studied.[4] It is clear that mass media can define, and sometimes force, a crisis on policymakers, who, being aware of this, seek to orchestrate media coverage in order to give themselves much room to maneuver, while yet keeping the public responsive to their initiatives. It has been stressed how

Rockefeller, particularly, performed the task of media orchestration superbly and how his departure and the crises after 1975 presented the media with considerable opportunities for more autonomy. In Dunn's terms, media input could then be maximized because *hard* decisions had to be faced and *new* policies had to be created by *new* officials.

The evidence of large media impact is incomplete. On the one hand, the media appeared to intensify the crisis over the New York City budget and also stimulated the Legislature to override a gubernatorial veto.[5] Clearly the media coverage of the Freedom of Information Act impasse helped resolve it as, likewise, did media coverage of Legislative expenses (the lulus) severely embarrass the legislative leadership and exacerbate conflicts within it.

Yet for many news writers the crisis situation after 1975 was illuminating on the *limitations* of media impact. The more dramatic the crisis, some reporters felt, the more they were kept out of the conflicts until resolutions had ben agreed on. One of the most influential members of the press corps commented: "Until 1975 I was inclined to overestimate our clout. When, however, I was kept outside the door for hours, given the outcome, and not told who was present, then I realized that when the chips really go down we're *just* observers. It was like a war situation." For him the episodes showed that media impact was restricted to relatively unimportant conflict situations in which media were *allowed* considerable, on occasion decisive, weight. This, of course, tends to confirm analyses of the Washington situation in which the media are managed, if not manipulated, more easily because it is easy for those in government to paint crises with a veneer of national security, highest national interest, and so on. At the state level this is much less possible—the questions are less "hot" in news terms—except when, as in New York after 1975, the viability of the State itself seemed in the balance.

In the eyes of some journalists, the impact of the press corps is lessened by its own lack of general competence. For them this is the important difference between Albany and Washington. We have already seen that Legislators and civil servants, rightly or wrongly, are inclined to agree with this point. Setting aside whether both groups wish media to have more impact, do they—and journalists too—feel that more training, preparation, and orientation would help?

Arguably, if the technical competence of journalists—their grasp of a field of surveillance—is questioned, then training and orientation might be a significant area of potential change.[6] Just over one-half of the reporters at Albany believed that they did not have enough training *before* entering journalism, and almost 40 percent of civil servants agreed. One-third of the legislators felt similarly, Democrats and Liberals being more ready to assert this as a need than Republicans and Conservatives.[a] Both legislators and civil servants were much more emphatic in their responses when asked specifically whether journalists needed more knowledge and training in politics and goverment at the State level. Here two-thirds of the legislators and four-fifths of the civil servants agreed, as—let it be said—did four-fifths of the journalists themselves.[b] As before, among legislators the Democrats and the Liberals seemed more sure of this than did the Republicans and the Conservatives. A desire for a knowledgeable, *trained* body of journalists accords with their earlier expressed attitudes on the significance of the mass media for both understanding government and mobilizing support behind changes they desire.

Clearly, there is a consensus on the need for journalists to be assisted by much more background information and formal orientation. Naturally enough, legislators and civil servants did not have pat answers to the question of what form this training should take. Nevertheless, more than half of both groups seemed to think that more study leave—sabbaticals at universities, travel grants, independent study—should be available to political journalists.[c] Republicans and, especially, Conservatives seemed to find the idea of a press corps better trained in this way to be irrelevant. Two of them made alternative suggestions. One, echoed by some reporters, was the notion that some journalistic ignorance and lack of perspective could be corrected by a period of attachment to a senior legislator and to one or two agencies. The other suggestion derived from the feeling that journalists become too jaded and routinized and ought to be taken off political journalism and put on other journalistic assignments. One legislator saw them as "too close, too blinkered, and too contemptuous—they *need* a change."

Among legislators and civil servants—and journalists, too—there is an occasionally lively dialogue over the consequences of the lack of or weakness in the education of journalists. One civil servant noted that "the nonspecialist tends to miss the salient . . . and emphasize the mundane and trivial." Another said bluntly, "You have to *know* and *understand* the language and the system before telling others about it." In this connection another civil servant urged ongoing seminars for journalists in the various policy areas and added, "The Southern Conference of Editors and Journalists is doing outstanding work along these lines."

Asked what steps could be taken to improve the information flow to the public, each group responded in terms of its own view of the shortcomings of the present situation. Thus, journalists mostly stressed the need for more access and more journalists. Interestingly, they seemed to believe that the Legislature would give more access before publishers would allow more journalists, and in this they appear to be correct. Democrats and Liberals, not surprisingly, stressed more access by journalists to the agencies; but of greater significance, others claimed, was greater access for themselves to the voters via the media—Conservatives and Republicans waxing the most strongly on this.[d] The clear preference of legislators for much less of an editorial role for the media is reflected here. For many legislators the independence of the mass media is a barrier to the flow of necessary political and governmental information to the public. For one, at least, the real answer lay in television—the magic medium in which, seemingly, the third party of the journalist was eliminated and on which a legislator might "be alone with his voters."

Civil servants clearly felt somewhat the same, though in relation to the agencies, not to the Governor or the Legislature. True to their technical orientation and their feeling that journalists were primarily ignorant, they mentioned the need for more coverage, but stressed the need for better journalists and less turnover among journalists—in short, a more qualified, stable press corps. The civil servants were less worried than journalists about familiarity's breeding contempt. For them familiarity breeds knowledge, "feel," and trust. Reporters on a short assignment in Albany are less likely to care about protecting their sources or even doing the work for a good story than the regulars, who will be back the next month, or the next day, and are aware of their need for goodwill. The opinion that public information would benefit from more and better public relations by the agencies had no general support, though one civil servant, clearly despairing of the press, noted that there should be "regular publication by the Governor to enumerate monthly the main activities of each department."

What was mentioned hardly at all by legislators, civil servants, or journalists was more *public* demand for information. Apart from particular need for greater access—for example, by candidates wishing to attack the record of incumbents or by public interest groups—the mass public clearly is seen as not involved very much and not likely to be. Perhaps for all three groups the larger public is not a notion that impinges on them very much. Each group has its target publics—legislators have their constituents; civil servants have their clientele groups; and reporters have their colleagues, editors, and a small fringe of attentive readers. Perhaps none of the groups retain the notion, if they ever had it, of the mass media as channels of constant, *general* political information of a kind that might help create and maintain an informed and mobilizable electorate. If the future holds the certainty of new, realigning issues, as legislators assert, then this notion might return in the minds of publishers, editors, and journalists to contest the ground currently so dominated by local, if not parochial, perspectives.

Reporters are well aware that legislators, too, can feel suffocated by the categorical imperatives of the local interest and the local view. Each group—the one for employment, and the other for reelection—feels unable to break out of the mold. Here television can be very important. It is not, as noted earlier, popularly labeled as partisan in the way that the local print press is and, potentially, might provide a vehicle for generating a higher level of statewide awareness that in turn could feed back from voters to journalists and legislators. Most of the Albany press corps believes that, generally, both the Governor and the legislators give easier access to television journalists; and we have seen how legislators regard television as the more valuable, *neutral* medium. In part this is true because, thus far, television coverage has been so thin and bland—a headline service with little analysis. The exception is the three-year-old PBS program "Inside Albany," whose arrival coincided with the revenue crisis and quickly generated an influential audience statewide. The program is widely respected—indeed, feared—for the careful intelligence that goes into its analysis and the good quality of its format and presentation. It is too early to say yet that it has affected television current-events programming overall in New York State. One index of such effect would be a decline in the certainty among legislators that television is somehow more neutral than the print press. Another index of effect would be a rise in the conviction among the Albany press corps that editors, near and far, want more than simply the "local angle" on the State—and more than just a steady reinforcement of their own *local* perspectives.

There is need for the media to be vehicles for ongoing dialogue between parties, groups, and sections. A bland, fence-sitting posture, with minimal commitment to explain State government and politics to the State's voters in ways that remind them of their larger loyalties, is in keeping with both larger American traditions and journalistic expectations. Myopic, self-interested dogmatisms that are still visible in the press, upstate and downstate, are offensive to those traditions. It may be comforting to readers to have their cherished ideas massaged and reinforced daily, but it may be dangerous to the polity not to encourage and support institutions that routinely question all received wisdom. Journalists see this as, classically, one of their more important functions and yet are only too aware that it is not one that is generally well performed. The training and resources of newswriters are very limited, as Edward Jay Epstein has pointed out.[7] This limitation becomes ever more glaring as governments engage in ever more complex decisions. One journalistic response, as we have seen, is to retreat into personalizing policy, into a pretense of covering *what* is at stake by supposedly covering *who* is in conflict or is likely to be. Another response —always present in the print press tradition and perhaps too much so today—is simply prescriptive: a retreat to so-called first principles even though the problems time and again are about the working out of those principles.

This brings us, finally, to the dimension of party and its significance. The Watergate episode showed how crucial a free press can be in the American system. The nation's founders, however, expected American liberties to be preserved as much—if not more—by contending factions as by a free press somehow divorced from that contention or existing above it. New York State has just emerged from a period in which a dominant Governor, Rockefeller, effectively managed or cowed both the political factions (parties) and the mass media. In consequence, image making proceeded apace and was unopposed. The legacy is evident in attitudes that this study has uncovered and discussed. Legislators, civil servants, and journalists in New York State are having to learn or relearn the complexities involved in *genuine* dialogues over policies, as opposed to the cosmetic consultation of earlier years. Thus, all groups are learning the limitations of their powers and influence and the necessity of harmonizing them. As the Legislature frees itself from excessive gubernatorial control externally and too much leadership control internally, as agencies and departments recover lost initiative, both legislators and civil servants take up again the burden of direct responsibility and occasionally long for the days when the Governor could be blamed for everything, whether he was leading or not.

Journalists, too, have greater freedom and greater responsibility than ever as they observe and report on the post-Rockefeller era. Their responsibilities are multifaceted and have inherent contradictions. Thus, journalists know that the public needs, and is entitled, to know both what government is doing and what groups inside and outside government say it is *not* doing, or not doing well. What government does or might do, anyway, is complex, and the process of translation of this complexity for the voters poses further problems. Thus, for reporters, to the limits of space are added the limits of their own and the public's comprehension and interest. Both limitations would be present whether or not journalists, newspapers, and radio and television stations were at times partisan.

Partisanship, as we have seen, is amply present, and the mass media, especially the newspapers, are vehicles and amplifiers of it. Indeed, newspapers and journalists often supply a coherence that seems lacking in the attitudes of both voters and their representatives. For this, they are often attacked by legislators, who see it as a challenge to their prerogative of setting the political agenda for New York State. The problem, of course, is solved not by such attacks, but by greater legislative coherence; and for that purpose the force of party needs reviving. Whether the present party structure is appropriate to the needs of New York State is, of course, a moot point—and one beyond the scope of this study. Journalists are as divided on the question as voters and are certain only that any realignment of loyalties would give them more work and more opportunity. That prospect both alarms and pleases the Albany press corps.

NOTES

1. Michael Kramer and Sam Roberts, *"I Never Wanted to be Vice President of Anything:"* An Investigative Biography of Nelson Rockefeller (New York: Basic Books, 1976), p. 170.

2. On this see Ken Norwick, "Making the News in the Capitol Press Room," *Empire State Report*, June 1976, pp. 171-72, 194-98; and Humphrey S. Tyler, "The LCA: An Institution Ripe for Reform," *Empire State Report*, June 1976, pp. 175-77.

3. Delmer Dunn, *Public Officials and the Press* (Reading, Mass.: Addison-Wesley, 1969).

4. On this, see Colin Seymour-Ure, *The Political Impact of Mass Media* (Beverly Hills, Calif: Sage Publications, 1974).

5. See Norwick, "Making the News," and Tyler, "The LCA," on this.

6. See Irving Kristol, "The Missing Elite," in George F. Will, ed., *Press, Politics and Popular Government* (Washington, D.C.: American Enterprise Institute for Public Policy Research, 1972). Also, for the change in journalistic attitudes, see Paul H. Weaver, "The New Journalism and the Old—Thoughts after Watergate," *Public Interest*, no. 35, Spring 1974, pp. 67-88.

7. Edward Jay Epstein, "Journalism and Truth," *Commentary* 57 (April 1974): 36-40

DATA

	Figures in parentheses	= n
	All others	= %
	Party Affiliation	Legislators only

a. Do you think journalists need more training—of whatever kind—*before* entering journalism?

	Yes	No	DK
Journalists	52.2 (12)	39.1 (9)	8.7 (2)
Legislators	30.0 (9)	43.3 (13)	26.7 (8)
C. Servants	38.9 (7)	38.9 (7)	22.2 (4)
Democrats	26.7 (4)	66.7 (10)	6.7 (1)
Republicans	33.3 (5)	20.0 (3)	46.7 (7)
Liberals	25.0 (2)	62.5 (5)	12.5 (1)
Conservatives	20.0 (2)	20.0 (2)	60.0 (6)

b. Do you think political journalists need a training in the nature and relevance of state politics?

	Yes	No	DK
Journalists	82.6 (19)	17.4 (4)	7.7 (2)
Legislators	69.2 (18)	23.1 (6)	4.5 (1)
C. Servants	81.8 (18)	13.6 (3)	
Democrats	91.7 (11)	8.3 (1)	
Republicans	50.0 (7)	35.7 (5)	14.3 (2)
Liberals	83.3 (5)	16.7 (1)	
Conservatives	60.0 (6)	20.0 (2)	20.0 (2)

c. If not, do you think they need more formal orientation and study leave?

	Yes	No	DK
Journalists	77.3 (17)	13.6 (3)	9.0 (2)
Legislators	63.6 (7)		36.3 (4)
C. Servants	53.8 (7)	15.4 (2)	30.8 (4)
Democrats	11.4 (5)	28.6 (2)	
Republicans	50.0 (2)	50.0 (2)	
Liberals	100.0 (4)		
Conservatives		100.0 (2)	

d. What changes, if any, do you think would contribute to the best kind of information flow to the public? [Mentions]

	Access	Information law	More journalists	More TV	More public demand	More legis-lative access to voters
Journalists	50.0 (10)	5.0 (1)	35.0 (7)	5.0 (1)		
Legislators	11.1 (2)	5.5 (1)	11.1 (2)			33.3 (6)
C. Servants	28.6 (4)	8.3 (3)	7.1 (1)		7.1 (1)	
Democrats	16.7 (2)		8.3 (1)			25.0 (3)
Republicans			16.7 (1)			50.0 (3)
Liberals	28.6 (2)					14.3 (1)
Conservatives			16.7 (1)			33.3 (2)

	More cover	Stable press corps	More P.R.	More papers	None
Journalists	5.5 (1)			5.0 (1)	
Legislators	28.6 (4)			11.1 (2)	22.2 (4)
C. Servants		21.4 (3)	7.1 (1)		33.3 (4)
Democrats	16.7 (1)			8.3 (1)	
Republicans				16.7 (1)	42.9 (3)
Liberals	16.7 (1)			14.3 (1)	16.7 (1)
Conservatives				16.7 (1)	

Epilogue—
The Carey
Administration

The material for this study was gathered during 1975 and 1976, when the new administration of Governor Hugh Carey was settling in to office amid a seemingly chronic fiscal crisis. That administration is now well past its halfway point. Indeed, thoughts about re-election in 1978 must be frequently in the minds of several of Carey's close friends and advisors. It is no longer a new administration, but one facing the need to renew its mandate.

With a three-year perspective is it possible to draw any conclusions about the differences in the quality of press-government relations in New York State? Has the Carey administration resulted in any changes in the quality of the relationship between journalists and the various parts of the government of New York State? As has been shown, newswriters *expected* Carey to behave differently toward them, and they certainly expected to behave differently toward him and, more generally, toward the agencies of government. The ghost of Rockefeller, they felt, needed exorcising. The centralization and control of the news supply in the Governor's office and its careful management for personal political ends were not so much to stop by order as they were to be found impossible to sustain, or so journalists hoped.

Only about one-quarter of the current members of the LCA were members when Rockefeller was Governor. A few others date from the early days of his successor, Malcolm Wilson. What follows is derived from conversations with those who remember Rockefeller. By and large, these are the more senior members of the LCA— guardians, as it were, of its received wisdom and significant actors in the socialization of newcomers to the press corps.

Has Carey made himself more accessible than Rockefeller? The answer clearly is no; indeed, two reporters think he has become even less accessible than Rockefeller was. The reasons given for this usually center, as one newsman noted, on the "siege mentality that developed after the pasting Carey rightly or wrongfully thought he had taken over issues such as New York City's financial troubles and the fiscal troubles of the state agencies." A symptom of this is that "he has almost no liaison with his press office" and prefers to make himself selectively available in New York City, where "he is more newsworthy than Rockefeller was because he's running things." Any good intentions Carey might have had, on this analysis, were overborne by the financial crisis. Only the prospect of re-election will force the Governor to try to change, to reduce his distance from the press.

If the accessibility of the Governor has changed little under Carey, what of the agencies? Earlier it was noted that as the Carey administration opened, there seemed some opportunity for a more independent agency stance vis-à-vis the press. Control by the Governor had meant for some agencies *less* possibility of more, and more open, press relations. Judged by the responses of newswriters, there has been some change in this area. The Freedom of Information Act has opened up some areas hitherto inaccessible, though, as one veteran commented, the act "has formalized the process so much that other things are less accessible." The act may have helped—even symbolically—but the real reason seems to be Carey's weakness and newness. As another newsman notes, Rockefeller "was more in control of the overall situation and . . . could instill a fear in the hearts of those in the various agencies. Carey has not developed the same kind of mastery, which helps reduce some of the barriers to investigating—potential sources are slightly more willing to talk." The logic in this suggests that if the current fiscal crises are resolved and if Carey is reelected, he will be able to control the agencies more easily, particularly in the area of their supply of news.

What of State news? Has the New York City crisis made the State level more visible to voters and its news more newsworthy for editors and readers? Here opinion seemed divided, with journalists stressing that while the New York City crisis has made big news, the State dimension of it had been too often submerged, even outside New York City proper. One newsman noted that the crisis: "perhaps has shifted the focus" of State news, exposing the vulnerability of the State to the chronic New York City crisis. Commenting on this shift, another said bluntly that the crisis has "muddled" the State dimension. Another—who saw not "muddle," but complexity, in the crisis—noted how it had been a means of educating voters to the importance of the State level. One of the most respected veterans noted that: "The *New York Times* and the A.P. have done some fine reporting on how and why the State government reacted to the crisis."

In any event, the newswriters are agreed that the volume of State level political and governmental news reported has changed little, if at all. What the New York City crises have done is to reduce the volume of other State news reported. Chronic crisis has its news limitation, and reporters are very aware of that. As one noted, "The stories of today are not very different from those we were writing a year ago—same subjects, almost the same substance. And that bores editors." Even if the crises were neither chronic nor severe, State news would not, for one newsman at least, have held great newsworthiness after Rockefeller. For him Carey has been short of money since his arrival in Albany, and this has prevented "the new kind of programs . . . [which could have] put his own stamp on government. Circumstances . . . have forced him to fight holding actions and give the impression of a defensive stance." By clear implication, stories of "gallant, dutiful defensive actions" by the Governor have a news appeal of strictly limited duration, however galling that might be to Governor Carey and those around him.

Has the relationship between the press and television been changed by the crisis atmosphere since 1974? Most journalists thought that the press role had been vindicated handsomely. Said one, "The New York City crisis is a perfect example of the weakness of broadcast news and the strength of the print media. The details of the story cannot be covered on the air-waves because of the complexities." Equally, perhaps more, important was the effect the crisis had in highlighting the dominant position of one newspaper in particular, namely, the *New York Times*. As one reporter put it, commenting on the recent past, "The resentment that most reporters felt . . . was that the administration ran its press operation almost exclusively for the *New York Times*. . . . [Reporters] rightly felt the *Times* was being favored on all stories rather than just those on the New York City crunch." If true, then it is a situation that any New York Governor would wish either to rectify or to mask. It also is a lead into a general assessment of the quality of the press-government relationship under Carey.

Given the Rockefeller inheritance, the prospective relationship between journalists and New York State government was not good when Carey took over. As has been noted, Rockefeller's successor, Malcolm Wilson, appeared stiff and distant and was a poor news maker. Carey's style was not much different at first, and the onset of the New York City crisis reinforced his predilecton for distance from reporters. Reflecting on the state of Carey's relations with the press, one newsman noted: "Rockefeller's people were more confident of their ability to manipulate the press. Carey's are neurotically antagonistic. Few of them will talk to reporters. The press office is kept deliberately uninformed about what the administration is doing and planning." In addition, Carey's press office has over the past months shown itself ready to criticize the reports of journalists in terms that are clearly meant to be intimidating. The Governor gives very few press conferences, and the coverage of his December 1976 conference led to public acrimony between some reporters and the press secretary, James T. Vlasto.

Relations have been slowly improving, but at best most reporters regard them as only fairly good and in need of much refurbishing. Reporters do not care for infrequent press conferences that need a second conference to provide "an explanation of what the Governor thought he had explained," as one put it. The resentments among reporters are only intensified by the favoritism shown to the *New York Times*. They have been told that this was a direct product of the New York City crisis. Claimed one reporter, the Carey staff reasoned that "bankers only read the *Times*. If the Carey course was to succeed, it had to appear in detail and correctly in the *Times*. The Carey people also were hoping for editorial support from the *Times*. They received it and believe it was more vital than anything else in inducing the bankers to go along." True or not, such an explanation has not particularly lessened journalistic frustration, not to say anger. One member of the Carey administration—Mario Cuomo, the Secretary of State—was singled out as trying to prevent further deterioration in press relations. Indeed, as one newsman observed, he became "just about every reporter's source on what was happening all over the government." This has helped but the situation is still far from satisfactory.

Press-government relations in New York State are thus in a trough of sorts. As noted earlier, reelection considerations may already be leading to energetic efforts to repair the relationships with reporters not on the *New York Times*. The victory of President Carter was expected to ease the New York City situation considerably, though, as of spring 1977, the fruits appear small and the reassurance tentative. If this situation is unchanged, the Governor is likely to continue to believe that retaining the editorial support of the *New York Times* and extending privileged access to its reporters are vital, even if the price is a chronic sourness elsewhere in the State press. Certainly few of these veteran journalists expect dramatic action from the President, though they concede that the situation has improved with the departure of Gerald Ford. A long crisis for New York City, therefore, is likely to continue the sour relations between the Governor and the Albany press corps, and his own reelection prospects could suffer as a result.

Bibliography

BOOKS

Balutis, Alan P., and Heaphey, James. *Public Administration and the Legislative Process.* Beverly Hills, Calif.: Sage Publications, 1974.

Berelson, B.; Gaudet, H.; and Lazarsfeld, P. F. *The People's Choice.* New York: Columbia University Press, 1948.

Berle, Peter A. A. *Does the Citizen Stand a Chance? Politics of a State Legislature: New York.* Woodbury, N.Y.: Barron's Educational Series, 1974.

Beyle, Thad, and Williams, J. Oliver, eds. *The American Governor in Behavioral Perspective.* New York: Harper & Row, 1972.

Blumler, Jay G., and Katz, Elihu, eds. *The Uses of Mass Communications: Current Perspectives on Gratifications Research.* Beverly Hills, Calif.: Sage Publications, 1974.

Blumler, Jay G. and McQuail, Denis. *Television in Politics.* Chicago: University of Chicago Press, 1963.

Brucker, Herbert. *Communication Is Power: Unchanging Values in a Changing Journalism.* New York: Oxford University Press, 1973.

Caldwell, Linton. *The Government and Administration of New York.* New York: Crowell, 1954.

Cash, Kevin. *Who the Hell is William Loeb?* Manchester, N.H.: Amoskeag Press, 1975.

Childs, Harwood L. *Public Opinion: Nature, Formation and Role.* Princeton, N.J.: D. Van Nostrand Co., 1965.

Cirino, R. *Power to Persuade: Mass Media and the News.* New York: Bantam Books, 1974.

Citizen's Conference on State Legislatures. *State Legislatures: An Evaluation of Their Effectiveness.* New York: Praeger, 1971.

Clarke, Peter, ed. *New Models for Mass Communication Research.* Beverly Hills, Calif.: Sage Publications, 1973.

Cohen, Bernard C. *The Press and Foreign Policy.* Princeton, N.J.; Princeton University Press, 1963.

Cohen, Stanley, and Young, Jack. *The Manufacture of News: A Reader.* Beverly Hills, Calif.: Sage Publications, 1973.

Connery, Robert H., and Benjamin, Gerald, eds. *Governing New York State: The Rockefeller Years.* Proceedings of the Academy of Political Science, vol. 31, no. 3, May 1974.

Cox, Harvey, and Morgan, David. *City Politics and the Press: Journalists and the Governing of Merseyside.* Cambridge: Cambridge University Press, 1973.

Danielson, W. A., ed. *Paul J. Deutschmann Memorial Papers in Mass Communications Research.* Cincinnatti: Scripps-Howard Research, 1963.

Deutsch, Karl. *The Nerves of Government: Models of Political Communication and Control.* Glencoe, Ill.: Free Press, 1966.

Diamond, Edwin. *The Tin Kazoo: Television, Politics and the News.* Cambridge, Mass.: M.I.T. Press, 1975.

Dunn, Delmer. *Public Officials and the Press,* Reading, Mass.: Addison-Wesley, 1969.

Easton, David. *A Systems Analysis of Political Life.* New York: John Wiley, 1965.

Ellul, Jacques. *The Political Illusion.* New York: Vintage Books, 1972.

Epstein, Edward Jay. *News from Nowhere: Television and the News.* New York: Random House, 1973.

Frank, Robert Shelby. *Message Dimension of Television News.* Lexington, Mass.: Lexington Books, 1973.

Frederickson, H. George, and O'Leary, Linda Schluter. *Power, Public Opinion and Policy in a Metropolitan Community: A Case Study of Syracuse, New York.* New York: Praeger, 1973.

Hawley, Willis D. *Nonpartisan Elections and the Case for Party Politics.* New York: John Wiley, 1973.

Hennessy, Bernard C. *Public Opinion.* Belmont, Calif.: Wadsworth, 1965.

Hevesi, Alan G. *Legislative Politics in New York State: A Comparative Analysis.* New York: Praeger, 1975.

Hiebert, R. E. *The Voice of Government.* New York: John Wiley, 1968.

Innis, Harold A. *The Bias of Communication.* Toronto: University of Toronto Press, 1951.

――――. *Empire and Communication.* Toronto: University of Toronto Press, 1972.

Janowitz, Morris. *The Community Press in an Urban Setting.* Chicago: University of Chicago Press, 1967.

Katz, Elihu, and Lazarsfeld, Paul F. *Personal Influence.* Glencoe, Ill.: Free Press, 1955.

Key, V. O., Jr. *Public Opinion and American Democracy.* New York: Alfred A. Knopf, 1965.

Kramer, Michael, and Roberts, Sam. *"I Never Wanted to be Vice President of Anything": An Investigative Biography of Nelson Rockefeller.* New York: Basic Books, 1976.

LeRoy, David J., and Sterling, Christopher H. *Mass News: Practices, Controversies and Alternatives.* Englewood Cliffs, N.J.: Prentice-Hall, 1973.

Lindzey, G., and Aronson, E., eds. *The Handbook of Social Psychology.* 5 Vols, Vol. 5. 2d ed. Reading, Mass.: Addison-Wesley, 1968.

McLuhan, Marshall. *The Gutenberg Galaxy.* Toronto: University of Toronto Press, 1962.

――――. *Understanding Media.* New York: McGraw-Hill, 1964.

Merrill, John C., and Barney, Ralph D. *Ethics and the Press: Readings in Mass Media Morality.* New York: Hastings House, 1975.

Merton, Robert K. *Mass Persuasion: The Social Psychology of a War Bond Drive.* New York: Harper, 1946.

Mickelson, Sig. *The Electric Mirror: Politics in the Age of Television.* New York: Dodd, Mead, 1972.

Morgan, David R., and Kirkpatrick, Samuel A., eds. *Urban Policy Analysis: A Systems Approach.* Glencoe, Ill.: Free Press, 1972.

Moscow, Warren. *Politics in the Empire State.* New York: Alfred A. Knopf, 1948.

New York Times. The Mass Media and Politics. New York: *New York Times,* 1972.

Nimmo, Dan D. *Newsgathering in Washington.* New York: Atherton Press, 1962.

Parenti, M. *Democracy for the Few.* New York: St. Martin's Press, 1974.

Pool, Ithiel de Sola, et. al. *The Prestige Press: A Comparative Study of Political Symbols.* Cambridge, Mass.: M.I.T. Press, 1970.

Rose, Richard. *Politics in England Today.* London: Faber and Faber, 1975.

Rosten, Leo C. *Washington Correspondents.* New York: Harcourt, Brace, 1937.

Rubin, Bernard. *Public Relations and the Empire State: A Case Study of*

New York State Administration, 1943-54. New Brunswick, N.J.: Rutgers University Press, 1958.

Sayre, Wallace A., and Kaufman, Herbert. *Governing New York City: Politics in the Metropolis.* New York: W. W. Norton, 1965.

Seiden, M. H. *Who Controls the Mass Media: Popular Myths and Economic Realities.* New York: Basic Books, 1974.

Seymour-Ure, Colin. *The Political Impact of Mass Media.* Beverly Hills, Calif.: Sage Publications, 1974.

Sigal, Leon V. *Reporters and Officials: The organization and politics of newsmaking.* Lexington, Mass.: D. C. Heath, 1973.

Stelzer Leigh, and Riedel, James A. *Capitol Goods: The New York State Legislature at Work.* Albany: G.S.P.A., S.U.N.Y., 1974.

Talese, Gay. *The Kingdom and the Power.* New York: World Publishing Co., 1969.

Viteritti, Joseph. *Police, Politics and Pluralism in New York City: A Comparative Case Study.* Beverly Hills, Calif.: Sage Publications, 1973.

Westerhof, Caroline S. *The executive connection: mayors and press secretaries, the New York experience.* Washington, D.C.: Dunellen, 1974.

Will, George F. ed. *Press, Politics and Popular Government.* Washington D.C.: American Enterprise Institute for Public Policy Research, 1972.

ARTICLES

Abelson, P. H. "Media Coverage of Substantive Issues." *Science* 184 (May 1974): 941.

Anson, R. S. "Rizzo and the Press: Kafkaesque Days in Philadelphia." *Columbia Journalism Review* 12 (May-June 1973): 44-49.

Awa, Nojoku E. "Communicating with the Rural Poor." *Journal of Extension* 12 (Winter 1974): 8-13.

Buckalew, James K. "The Local Radio News Editor as a Gatekeeper." *Journal of Broadcasting* 18 (Spring 1974): 211-21.

Clarke, Peter, and Kline, Gerald. "Media Effects Reconsidered: Some New Strategies for Communication Research." *Communication Research,* April 1974, p. 224-40.

Coffey, Philip J. "A Quantitative Measure of Bias in Reporting of Political News." *Journalism Quarterly* 52 (Autumn 1975): 551-52.

Counts, Tilden M. "The Influence of Message and Source on Selection of Statements by Reporters." *Journalism Quarterly* 52 (Autumn 1975): 443-49.

Cranberg, Gilbert. "Mail Survey Respondents and Non-Respondents." *Journalism Quarterly* 52 (Autumn 1975): 542-43.

Dreyer, Edward C. "Media Use and Electoral Choices: Some Political Consequences of Information Exposure." *Public Opinion Quarterly* 35 (Winter 1971-72): 544-53.

Epstein, Edward Jay. "Journalism and Truth." *Commentary* 57 (April 1974): 36-40.

Jennings, Kent, and Ziegler, Harmon. "The Salience of American State Politics." *American Political Science Review* 64 (June 1970): 523-35.

Katz, Elihu. "Two Step Flow of Communication." *Public Opinion Quarterly* 21 (1957): 61-78.

McClure, Robert D., and Patterson, Thomas E. "Television News and Political Advertising: The Impact of Exposure to Voter Beliefs." *Communication Research,* January 1974, p. 3-31.

Manheim, Jarol B. "Urbanization and Differential Press Coverage of the Congressional Campaign: Analysis of Coverage by 26 Papers in Five Midwestern Districts in 1970 Campaign Shows Quantity and Quality Vary Systematically with Degree of Urbanization." *Journalism Quarterly* 51 (Winter 1974): 649-53.

Mott, George Fox. "Communication Turbulence in Urban Dynamics: Media, Education and Planning." *Annals* 405 (January 1973): 114-30.

Norwick, Ken. "Making the News in the Capitol Press Room." *Empire State Report,* June 1976, p. 171-72, 194-98.

Roshwalb, I., and Resnicoff, L. "Impact of Endorsements and Published Polls on the 1970 New York Senatorial Election." *Public Opinion Quarterly* 35 (Fall 1971): 410-14.

Rukeyser, Louis, "How the Press Helped New York Go Broke." *More,* 5 September 1975, p. 6.

Tichenor, P. J., and Wackman, D. B. "Mass Media and Community Public Opinion." *American Behavioral Scientist* 16 (March-April 1973): 593-606.

Tichenor, P. J., et al. "Community Issues, Conflict, and Public Affairs Knowledge." In *New Models for Mass Communication Research,* ed. P. Clarke. Beverly Hills, Calif.: Sage Publications, 1973.

Tyler, Humphrey S. "The LCA: An Institution Ripe for Reform." *Empire State Report,* June 1976, p. 175-77.

U. S. Government, *Government Reports Announcements, Media and Local Government: A San Francisco Bay Area Study.* No. 22, Group 5D, 1974.

U. S. Government, *Government Reports Announcements, The Use of*

Mass Media by Local and Regional Governments. No. 6, Group 5B, 1975.

Weaver, Paul H. "The New Journalism and the Old—Thoughts after Watergate." *Public Interest* 35, Spring 1974, p. 67-88.

Weiss, Carol H. "What America's Leaders Read." *Public Opinion Quarterly* 38 (Spring 1974): 1-22.

DISSERTATIONS

Bell, Lillian Smith. "The Role and Performance of Black and Metro Newspapers in Relation to Political Campaigns in Selected, Racially-Mixed Congressional Elections, 1960-1970." Ph.D. diss., Northwestern University, 1974.

Brownstein, Charles Nathan. "The Effect of Media, Message, and Interpersonal Influence on the Perception of Political Figures." Ph.D. diss., Florida State University, 1971.

Einsiedel, Edna Flores. "Reporter-Source Orientation, Source Attraction, Topic Importance, and Reporter Information-Seeking Behavior." Ph.D. diss., Indiana University, 1975.

Englehardt, Robert W. "Freedom of Information Law in New York State: Status and Recent Developments." M.A. thesis, Marquette University, 1974.

Golderberg, Edie Nan. "The Access of Resource-Poor Groups to the Metropolitan Press." Ph.D. diss., Stanford University, 1974.

Hale, Edward. "Newsmen and Government Men: A Study of the Interaction and Role Behavior of Professional Communicators Involved in the Transmission of Information from Executive Agencies in New York State Government to the Newspaper Reading Public." Ph.D. diss., G.S.P.A., S.U.N.Y., Albany, 1966.

Hevesi, Alan G. "Legislative Leadership in New York State." Ph.D. diss., Columbia University, 1971.

Jones, David William, Jr. "The Press and the Politics of Urban Growth: A Study of Cues and Constraints in the Politicized Newsroom." Ph.D. diss., Stanford University, 1974.

Nexon, David. "Party, Public Opinion, and Policy Formation: The Dynamics of Representation." Ph.D. diss., University of Chicago, 1974.

Palmgreen, Philip Charles. "Mass Communication and Political Knowledge: The Effects of Political Level and Mass Media Coverage on Political Learning." Ph.D. diss., University of Michigan, 1975.

Roche, Bruce Ware. "The Effect of Newspaper Owners' Non- Media Business Interests on News Judgments of Members of News Staffs." Ph.D. diss., Southern Illinois University, 1975.

Weber, Robert P. "Party and Committees in the New York State Assembly." Ph.D. diss., University of Rochester, 1975.

Wiggins, Robert Gene. "Access to the Mass Media: Public's Right or Publisher's Privilege?" Ph.D. diss., Southern Illinois University, 1973.

Index

Adirondack Enterprise, 18, 20, 21, 22
Albany *Knickerbocker News,* 19, 20, 21, 22, 82, 134
Albany *Times Union,* 19, 20, 21, 22, 82, 134
Anderson, Senator Warren, 40

Berelson, B., 6
Berle, Assemblyman Peter A. A., 38
Binghamton *Sun-Bulletin,* 19, 20, 21, 22
Buffalo, New York, ix
Buffalo *News,* 18, 19, 20, 21, 22

Carey, Governor Hugh A., viii, 29, 46
  journalistic assessment of, 161-65
Christian Science Monitor, 134
Civil servants
  age, education, and experience of, 56-58

  on journalistic training, 152-54
  on journalists, 82-91, 123-24
  on media roles, 62-69
  on New York State government, 58-62, 122
  on Rockefeller, 45-49
Coalition for Legislative Reform, 38
Conservative Party, 60
Common Cause, 38
Coulter, Philip, 4

Daily News. See New York Daily News
Dewey, Governor Thomas E., 28, 34-35
Dunn, Delmer, 149
Duryea, Assemblyman Perry, 40

Ellul, Jacques, 4
Epstein, Edward Jay, 155

Frank, R. S., 6-7
Freedom of Information Act 1976
  history of, 37-39, 151

Gaudet, H., 6
Gleason, Eugene, 30
Governor's Office and mass media, 124-25
Greenberg, B. S., 6

Herald-Journal. See Syracuse *Herald-Journal*

Information Flow Models, 6-9
Innis, Harold A., 4

Journalists
  age, education, and experience of, 56-58
  on interest groups, 107
  on investigative journalism, 105
  on legislators and civil servants, 99-111, 125-27
  on media roles, 62-69
  on political parties, 107
  on public relations, 108-10
  on Rockefeller, 43-47

Katz, Elihu, 6-7
Kaufman, Herbert, 4
Knickerbocker News. See Albany *Knickerbocker News*

Lazarsfeld, P. F., 6
Legislative Correspondents Association, ix
Legislators
  age, education, and experience of, 45-49
  on journalistic training, 152-54
  on journalists, 82-91
  on media roles, 62-69
  on New York State government, 58-62, 120-21
  on Rockefeller, 45-49

Lehman, Governor Herbert, 28
Liberal Party, 60

McLuhan, Marshall, 4
Media Effects, 7-9
Moscow, Warren, 26-29

News. See Buffalo *News*
Newsday, 18, 20, 21, 22, 82, 106
News editors
  age and background of, 133
  on journalists, 138
  on news bias, 142-44
  on New York State government, 136-37
  on New York State news, 136-37
  on Watergate, 141
Newsweek, 134
New York City, viii, ix
New York Daily News, 18, 20, 21, 22, 82
New York Post, 82
New York State government
  editors and aides on, 136-37
  gubernatorial style of, 27-30
  legislative leadership style of, 30-34
  public relations staffs of, 34-39
New York State mass media, 16
  press content of, 18-23
New York State news
  editors and aides on, 136
New York Times, 3, 18, 64, 68, 82, 84, 87, 89, 91, 103, 106, 134, 143, 163-65

Post. See New York Post
Post-Standard. See Syracuse *Post-Standard*
Public Broadcasting System, ix, 139

Public Relations Aides
   age and background of, 133-34
   on journalists, 138
   on news bias, 142-44
   on New York *Times,* 139
   on New York State news and
      government, 136-37
   on Watergate, 141

Riedel, James A., 30, 33
Rochester, New York, ix
Rockefeller, Governor Nelson A.,
      vii, 28, 35-36
   civil servants on, 45-49
   journalists on, 43-47
   legislators on, 45-49
   news editors and aides on, 135
   news legacy, 147-48
Roosevelt, Governor Franklin D., 28
Rose, Richard, 4

Sayre, Wallace A., 4
Seymour-Ure, Colin, 7
Sigal, Leon, 3
Smith, Governor Alfred E., 28

Stelzer, Leigh, 30, 32
Sun-Bulletin. See Binghamton *Sun-
   Bulletin*
Syracuse, New York, ix
Syracuse *Herald-Journal,* 19, 20,
      21, 22
Syracuse *Post-Standard,* 19, 20,
      21, 22

Time, 134
Times. See New York Times;
   Watertown *Times*
Times Union. See Albany *Times
   Union*

Urban Development Corporation,
   viii

Vlasto, James T., 164

Wall Street Journal, 82, 134
Washington Post, 3, 68, 141
Watertown *Times,* 19, 20, 21, 22
Wilson, Governor Malcolm, vii,
      29, 40, 46, 161, 164

Zimmerman, Joseph, 30

ABOUT THE AUTHOR

David Morgan is Senior Lecturer in the Department of Politics at The University in Liverpool, England. He specializes in American government and mass media, and has published several books and articles on media, women's suffrage, and politics.